M000158170

"As a pastor, I suspect that we exempt ourselves too often from what we expect from others every Sunday: to wrestle with truth, to risk reflection, and to choose growth. Dr. McKinney gently *shepherds the shepherds,* holding a mirror to our exposed parts. She distills rich experience, psychological insight, and scholarship, and offers us the 'gift of interpretation'—about the transience of our members, their spiritual vacancy, and ultimately their absence from our pews. This book offers pastors a palatable condensation of what our members have long discussed in parking lots, after benedictions. What greater gift can we receive than voices from the pew—while they still love us enough to stay and talk. Even if the conversation is difficult to hear, preachers, it is imperative that we listen and live the 'AMEN!'"

—*Rev. Dr. Claudette Anderson Copeland*
pastor, New Creation Christian Fellowship, San Antonio, TX
and author of Stories from Inner Space: Confessions of a
Preacher Woman and Other Tales

. . .

"Any preacher who takes seriously the craft of preaching is well aware of the need to exegete Scripture and context, which provide content for sermonic proclamation. Dr. McKinney gives to us what our sermons look like (how people view and interpret the vessel speaking) and often sound like (what the pew really hears). This book is valuable for keeping fresh and positive dialogue between pulpit and pew."

—*Rev. Dr. William Curtis*
senior pastor, Mount Ararat Baptist Church, Pittsburgh, PA
and vice president, Hampton University Ministers' Conference

. . .

"Dr. Lora-Ellen McKinney's latest offering is a tender and loving blessing to people of faith and those who serve them as preachers of the Christian gospel. Her direct style, clear language, and poignant examples make the book easy to read and a joy to think about. Preachers, pastors, pulpit selection committees, seminary students, and people who love preaching and preachers will find themselves nodding in agreement with Dr. McKinney's observations and insights. Many of the insights and observations are drawn from her experience as daughter of Dr. Samuel Berry McKinney, one of the visionary preachers of our time. Others arise from careful research and studied questioning of parishioners and preachers about the dynamics that take place between preachers and those in the pew—or which fail to occur—during preaching efforts.

Preachers, read this book before you deliver too many more sermons. Parishioners, read this book before you hear too many more sermons. *For the love of the gospel of God's redemptive love and its proclamation through preaching, READ THIS BOOK!"*

—*Rev. Wendell L. Griffen*
parliamentarian, National Baptist Convention, USA, Inc.
and coordinator of ministries,
Mount Pleasant Baptist Church, Little Rock, AR

• • •

"Lora-Ellen McKinney has provided a much-needed resource that will be as beneficial for the people seated in the pews as it will be for those who will be standing behind the pulpit. She reminds us all that both parties are engaged in ministry together, and that the thoughts, perceptions, and expectations of the people who hear the sermons and observe the pastor at work should not be ignored or overlooked. This book is helpful for preachers because it provides a mirror in which we can catch a reflection of ourselves as we perform our various pastoral tasks. This book is equally helpful for people in the pew because it empowers and encourages them to expect the very best from their pastors and preachers. Not since *A Voice From the Crowd* by George Wharton Pepper, one of the few non-clerics to give the Lyman Beecher Lectures on Preaching at Yale Divinity School in 1914, has a book been written that has tried to reflect on how preachers are perceived by those who observe them at work week after week. This book is a gift to the church!"

—*Rev. Dr. Marvin A. McMickle*
senior pastor, Antioch Baptist Church, Cleveland, OH
and author of An Encyclopedia of African American Christian Heritage

• • •

"Wow! ... This book should be required reading for all seminarians and pastors. Dr. McKinney has done a great service for the body of Christ by sharing with the pulpit the view of the 'word and preacher' from the perspective of the pew. Her practical advice will assist any developing minister in the area of homiletics and teaching and inspire within them a desire to be clear, relevant, and loving from the pulpit. Do not mistake the author's passion for the church as criticism without love. This book is a beautifully written love letter to pastors from a committed Christian and lifelong 'PK.' Make room on your bookshelf for this book!"

—*Rev. Dr. Otis B. Moss III*
senior pastor, Tabernacle Baptist Church, Augusta, GA

view from the pew

LORA-ELLEN McKINNEY

view from the pew

What Preachers Can Learn
from Church Members

Judson Press
Valley Forge

View from the Pew: What Preachers Can Learn from Church Members
© 2004 by Judson Press, Valley Forge, PA 19482-0851
All rights reserved.

No part of this publication may be reproduced, stored in a retrieval system, or trans-
mitted in any form or by any means, electronic, mechanical, photocopying, recording,
or otherwise, without the prior permission of the copyright owner, except for brief
quotations included in a review of the book.

Judson Press has made every effort to trace the ownership of all quotes. In the event
of a question arising from the use of a quote, we regret any error made and will be
pleased to make the necessary correction in future printings and editions of this book.

Bible quotations in this volume are from *The Holy Bible,* King James Version (KJV).
The author notes that she is particularly fond of the King James Version's lyrical language
and finds beauty and comfort in its words.

The author and Judson Press would like to express sincere gratitude to GIA Publications, Inc., Chicago, Illinois, for their permission to reprint many of the songs
contained therein. As specified in the notes, those selections are from the *African
American Heritage Hymnal* (2001), edited by Rev. Dr. Delores Carpenter and Rev.
Nolan E. Williams Jr.

Library of Congress Cataloging-in-Publication Data

McKinney, Lora-Ellen.
  View from the pew : what preachers can learn from church members /
Lora-Ellen McKinney.
        p. cm.
  Includes bibliographical references.
  ISBN 0-8170-1459-4 (alk. paper)
  1. Preaching.   I. Title.
BV4211.3.M36 2004
251--dc22

                                                                        2003070702

Printed in the U.S.A.

10 09 08 07 06 05 04

10 9 8 7 6 5 4 3 2 1

Don't exalt the preacher,
Don't exalt the pew,
Preach the Gospel simple, full and free;
Prove Him and you will find that promise is true,
"I'll draw all men unto Me." *

* Johnson Oatman Jr., "Lift Him Up," in *African American Heritage Hymnal,* ed. Delores Carpenter and Nolan E. Williams Jr. (Chicago: GIA Publications, 2001), 547. Copyright © by GIA Publications, Inc., Chicago, Illinois. All rights reserved. Used with permission.

contents

To the Rev. Dr. Samuel Berry McKinney,
the first preacher, minister, religion teacher,
spiritual guide, and pastor in my life,
and my beloved father.
You serve as a model
from whom others should learn,
and in learning,
would serve their church members well.

foreword

DR. LORA-ELLEN MCKINNEY HAS WRITTEN ONE OF THE MOST INSIGHT-
ful and helpful books on homiletics that perhaps has ever been
written by a non-practitioner of the craft of preaching. Most of
the "must-read" volumes on the art of preaching are written by
names that are familiar with both homileticians and seminarians.
Books like Buttrick's *Homiletic*, Fred Craddock's *Preaching*,
Joseph Johnson's *Proclamation Theology* and *The Soul of the
Black Preacher*, C. Eric Lincoln's *The Black Experience and
Religion*, and Henry Mitchell's *Black Preaching* and *The
Recovery of Preaching* are books most African American
ministers know from start to finish. Books like Katie Can-
non's *Teaching Preaching* and Frank Thomas's *They Like to
Never Quit Praisin' God*, Samuel DeWitt Proctor's *Preaching
On Crisis in the Community*, *My Moral Odyssey*, and *We
Have This Ministry* (co-authored with Gardner Taylor),
James A. Forbes's *The Holy Spirit and Preaching*, and Gardner C. Taylor's *How Shall They Preach?* are books that most
students find on their required reading lists when they take a
course in homiletics. Those books are "standard stock" text-
books for any man or woman of the gospel who would dare
to stand and face the people of God on a Sunday morning.

Professors of homiletics all over this country, especially in the
five fully-accredited (ATS) African American seminaries, use

these volumes to help their students learn the basics of homiletics and the importance of all of the mechanics when it comes to preparing a sermon and preaching a sermon. All of these works are excellently written, well thought out, and extremely important for anyone who would dare to try to be a spokesperson for the awesome God whose Word and will are found within the sacred texts that we call the Holy Scriptures.

All of them, however, are written by practitioners of the craft. They are written by persons who teach (or taught) preaching, and for that reason they are invaluable when it comes to understanding all of the aspects concerning that "holy moment" when the messenger of God dares to speak a Word from God.

Dr. McKinney's volume, however, is the first book that I have run across that is written by a non-practitioner! Dr. McKinney is neither a minister of the gospel, a preacher of the gospel, a student of homiletics, or a teacher of homiletics. Dr. McKinney writes from the vantage point of a layperson. That makes her volume invaluable from my perspective. I speak both as a pastor and as a professor of homiletics when I make this assessment.

Dr. McKinney writes about how the preacher of the gospel should be prepared to preach, how she or he should celebrate the centrality of Christ in the preaching moment, and how the preacher should be ultimately concerned that the "Word" they are preaching is God's Word and not his or her *own* words. She also stresses the importance for pastors of being a shepherd to the flock to whom they preach, or as Dr. James Cone says, "the importance of exegeting the congregation!"

Being a pastor does not mean being six feet above the persons to whom one preaches. Dr. McKinney points out that it means being (in Gardner Taylor's words), "A person from their own coasts!" Dr. Taylor uses the imagery found in the Book of Ezekiel where God tells the people to choose a watchman from their own coasts, one who lives in the city where they live, as one who would stand on the wall and cry out when the enemy approaches. A person who is invested in the lives and the community where he or she is serving as one of them and not one *above* them will preach sermons that hit home in a way that excellent exercises in oratory will never hit home! Dr. McKinney builds on Dr. Taylor's advice and urges all who would dare to preach the gospel to expose the pastor in themselves by showing how they are a person "from the coasts" of those whom they serve.

As a layperson, Dr. Lora-Ellen McKinney gives advice to those of us in ministry that is very practical, very helpful, and deeply spiritual. She reminds us of the importance of vision ("Where there is no vision, the people perish"), the continuity of tradition, and the value of standing on the shoulders of those who have come before us, while reminding us of what it means to be a part of the "family of faith."

In almost every middle income African American family (or those whom Marvin McMickle would call the "Black Middle Class"), there is a wide variety of backgrounds and experiences— all in the same family! There are persons in the family like Dr. McKinney who have an earned Ph.D. and there are persons in that same family who did not finish grammar school. The letters behind a person's name are things that make family members proud. They do not, however, entitle that person to some degree of exalted esteem not shared by the matriarch or patriarch of that family who did not finish grammar school. Those letters behind a name don't matter in that fashion when it comes to the African American concept and understanding of "family."

Dr. McKinney reminds us that the same principles hold true when it comes to the family of God. There are persons who we in ministry face each week who are highly educated, and there are also persons sitting right next to them who have not been as fortunate as those of us who have been blessed to go to college and graduate school. They all are God's children. They all are equal in God's sight and they all come Sunday after Sunday to hear a word from the Lord. Those who dare to preach must speak to every level of humankind (academically, sociologically, economically, and spiritually), and we must do so each week (and at each opportunity) with the understanding that we speak to persons who are "hungry for the living bread!"

The Ga-Dangme people of Ghana taught me the lesson that Dr. McKinney stresses when they pointed out that under the sandals of every chief there lies a lamb's skin. The lambskin is a symbol of humility because the chief (or the preacher) must remember that he or she is addressing persons who are highly educated and persons who are uneducated, and he or she must speak to all of them with the same degree of love, compassion, and care. The only way to do that is to remain humble!

There are many persons in ministry who might react negatively to reading a volume on preaching that is written by one who is not a practitioner of preaching. Let me explain to those persons in particular and to the other readers in general why I argue in favor of this tremendous work that Dr. Lora-Ellen McKinney has written.

Dr. McKinney writes first of all as a woman who loves God, a woman who loves the Word of God, and a woman who loves the people of God. She does not write as an "outsider" to the black religious experience. She is the daughter of one of America's leading African American pastors, the Rev. Dr. Samuel McKinney, and she is the granddaughter of the Rev. Dr. Wade Hampton McKinney II.

Lora-Ellen grew up in the church. Her spiritual roots were planted deep in the soil of the African American religious experience. Her parents and grandparents led her to the Lord, and she is a woman who loves the Lord with all of her heart, soul, and *mind!*

Reading a book on preaching written by a layperson who loves the Lord is a unique experience. Reading a book written by a layperson who is a trained psychologist adds yet another dimension to what it means to truly love the Lord our God with all of our hearts, souls, and minds!

Dr. McKinney is also a woman who loves the Word of God. Clinically trained in the works of Freud and Jung, she is deeply grounded in her profession as a clinician. As a child of God, however, she is also deeply grounded in the "Living Word," which feeds those inner recesses of her soul—places that cannot be reached by academia alone. Her love for the Word of God gives her an appreciation for preaching and a "critical ear" when listening to preaching that many parishioners do not have.

Many "Preacher's Kids" have such negative experiences in the church that they end up not liking the people of God! Lora-Ellen is an awesome exception to that rule. She is a "P.K." who loves the people of God. Her love for the people of God gives her an appetite for the preached word that covets sermonic excellence and substance for all who gather on a Sunday to hear from heaven.

Lora-Ellen also writes this book from the perspective of a woman who cares for the church. She cares for the local congregation. She cares for the church universal. She cares for the broken body of Christ in all of its current manifestations: racism, sexism, heterosexism, homophobia, its ignoring HIV/AIDS, and its fixation on classism. She also cares deeply about the feeding of the congregation. It is Dr. McKinney's view from the pew that every time the people of God gather they should be fed the Word of God, fed the Bread of Heaven, and fed lovingly, carefully, and with integrity. When you read her thoughts on sermonic preparation and congregational expectation, you will see why she has such a deep passion for the adequate feeding of the people of God every time they gather in the House of God.

As a clinical psychologist and an ordained deacon, Dr. McKinney also brings to this work a perspective that demonstrates a care for the spiritual growth of the congregation. Dr. Isaac Clark, the former professor of homiletics at the Interdenominational Theological Center in Atlanta, said that people flock to Billy Graham because they are "being fed" there. They flock to crusades that Billy Graham holds, that T. D. Jakes holds, and that many other "mass media ministers" hold, because they are "getting fed" there. Dr. Clark says they are getting fed at those crusades and they are not "getting fed" at their local churches.

The problem that Dr. Clark lifts up is that in far too many instances the members of thousands of congregations are flocking to hear their "media ministers" because at those crusades they are getting fed *what they like to eat!* Children like ice cream and cake. Children love peach cobbler and sweet potato pie. Children would much rather have the things they *like* to eat than the things that they *need* to eat. Unfortunately, any dietician will tell you that what folk *like* to eat and what they *need* to eat are two different things entirely. What they like to eat might stunt their growth and cause them to be deformed. The same is true when it comes to spiritual food and the spiritual growth that is necessary in a congregation.

Dr. Lora-Ellen McKinney cares about the spiritual food that will cause growth and feed the flock of God what they need to eat and not just what they like to eat! Her advice and her encouragement to preachers and to parishioners in this volume illustrate this point magnificently.

I ultimately urge this book on preaching to those of us who practice this profession weekly because it is written by a layperson who embraces the marriage between the head and the heart, one who embraces the marriage between the intellect and emotions, and one who is excited about preaching and has high expectations from those who preach week after week!

Because of the North Atlantic Theological Education model, far too many of us were raised in far too many instances in a tradition that puts the head and the heart at odds with one another. We were raised (in the black religious tradition) with an understanding that one either had to be seminary trained or one had to be "called." The emphasis, far too often, was placed on the "call" and not on the preparation academically that came after the call for the serving of "this present age."

That kind of dichotomous thinking caused a bifurcation within the spiritual life of African Americans that was never there biblically. Jesus said that there is no separation between thinking and feeling. When asked what the greatest commandment was, Jesus quoted Leviticus and said that we are to *love* the Lord our God, and love is an emotion! He said we are to love the Lord our God with all of our hearts and souls. That is pure emotion!

Jesus also says, however, something that the passage in Leviticus does not say. Jesus says that we are to love the Lord our God with all of our *minds!* That marries the head and heart. That marries the intellect and emotions, and Dr. McKinney—a trained layperson who loves the Lord—brings that expectation to church with her Sunday after Sunday as she sits and waits to hear from heaven.

This book on preaching is written by a woman who is excited about the preaching event! So many laypeople in the opening days of the Twenty-first Century are shallow when it comes to homiletics, to exposition, to exegesis, and to integrity in the preached moment. They are what I call "Praise-A-Holics." They are heavily into praise and worship. They couldn't care less about "content" when it comes to the Word of God being preached with integrity and being preached within the context of African American life in the opening days of a century in which the "color problem" (to quote DuBois) is still not solved! The expectation for far too many shallow parishioners is to hear some trite phrases and to focus in on the "style" of a preacher and not be concerned about any substance.

Dr. McKinney breaks the mold. She calls to task those of us who would dare stand to proclaim the "unsearchable riches" of the gospel of Jesus Christ. She challenges us to be faithful in our treatment of the text and our speaking to the context within which the people whom we serve live on a day-to-day basis. She cares about content! She cares about substance—not just style.

Dr. McKinney cares about integrity, and she is excited about the preaching of the gospel because she cares so deeply. She expects those of us who represent the One who lived a life of integrity to have no less integrity when it comes to being faithful to the call that he has placed upon our lives.

Dr. McKinney's book should be placed on the shelves of our libraries right next to Henry Mitchell's, Frank Thomas's, Sam Proctor's, and Gardner Taylor's. I believe this volume should be placed there and referred to often after having been read, digested, and internalized! I thank God for this woman of God who has made an invaluable contribution to the field of homiletics in the opening days of the Twenty-first Century.

Dr. Jeremiah A. Wright Jr.
Senior Pastor
Trinity United Church of Christ, Chicago, Illinois

introduction

I DECIDED TO WRITE THIS BOOK FOR VERY PERSONAL REASONS. Among the first loves in my life was my love for a preacher, an amazing man—the Rev. Dr. Samuel Berry McKinney— whom I am honored to call Daddy. From observing his circle of friends and a vast array of ministers, male and female, and through a life spent seeking God's presence and purpose for my life, I have learned an amazing amount about the perspective that the "pew-sitter" has on the pastorate. Based on a lifetime of church attendance, of looking from the pew to the pulpit for spiritual sustenance and inspiration, and of listening to the comments of parishioners that fall just to the left of "Amen!" I have a wealth of information to share with preachers that I think can enhance the ways that they preach, administer, and pastor and thus strengthen the corporate worship relationship that they seek to create on Sunday mornings and in which we parishioners wish to be active participants.

Worship is, after all, about both perspectives: the viewpoint of the pastor observing and interacting with the flock, and the experience of parishioners who watch, wait, and worship from the pew. In conjunction with all of the ministries that participate to bring meaning to worship, pastor and parishioner engage in a meaningful relationship, one that determines the size of the congregation, the power of the minister in the local community, and the creation of a spiritual aura that surrounds the purpose and the passion of what we experience as "church."

The most important reason for writing this book is related to my love for God. The longer I live, the more important it becomes to me to that, as the psalmist prays to God, "the words of my mouth and the meditations of my heart be acceptable in your sight." As a result, I experience worship on many levels. I observe the behaviors of the congregation in response to the various components of worship. I pay attention to *my* responses. On any particular Sunday, what moves me to tears and opens my heart? Or what confuses my spirit? I listen carefully to the preached word. I pay attention to the intent of the message, the consistency of the content, the strength of the points that are made, the relevance of the topic to my life, and the ways in which I might use what I have learned in a practical way. This, I think, is the purpose of preaching—to inspire, to teach, to honor, to praise, and to move God's people to action.

Worship celebrates our relationship with God. It is a weekly opportunity to exalt God with our praise, to honor him with our prayers, to celebrate him through song, and to learn about his Word through the powerful process of preaching. Preaching is a moment of intimacy in the worship celebration; it ushers into being an instant in time where God speaks to us from history and acts upon us in the present.

I admit to making an assumption here that most parishioners want what I want from the preaching experience. Having said that, I do understand that my perspective differs somewhat from that of most parishioners. It results, I am certain, from being the child of a minister. My minister was my pastor *and* my father—a difficult task for him and an occasionally confusing relationship process for me. I worried about the dichotomy of my father's roles. For example, if I admitted wrongdoing to him, would he be my pastor and help me seek God's forgiveness, or would he be my father and discipline me? Another confusion was this: most parishioners heard my father only on Sundays or when they chose to be at church or at our home. I heard my father talk all the time and in every single aspect of my life—at home, in the car, when I did well, when I was in trouble (a rare experience!), on early morning Saturday radio in Seattle (Bible lessons), on late-night television ads for the Council of Churches, on Sunday mornings at 10:45 and then as part of my father's Sunday afternoon self-assessment, on tape recordings of the sermon I had just heard in church that morning.

So I started listening to sermons with a critical ear. Critical does not mean negative in this context. Rather, I listened carefully, giving my father feedback on the strength of a particular sermon or noting how the congregation was moved by his tears when he talked about a subject close to his heart. I let him know when he promised to talk about three issues and broached only two. I praised him when he, sensing a shift in the corporate experience of the Spirit of God on an especially anointed Sunday morning, let the moving ministry of song substitute for the sermon. This critical listening ear is very much a part of me; it is strongly related to the reason that I became a psychologist. My gift is listening to words and to what is behind them, for understanding their lyricism and potential power, and for seeing the ways in which they are strengthened or diminished by behavior.

In recent years seminaries and homiletics scholars have bemoaned the decline of the "art of the sermon." Their concern is that in too many cases sermons are more conversation than theological treatise, more performance than oratory, more style than content. I know and love ministers. I have been around them all of my life and have had the marvelous opportunity to sit at the feet of many of the greatest preachers, religious scholars, and teachers of the last few generations. Yet I must say that some of the highly publicized critiques seem true. My comments are not focused on the pastoral "bad sermon day," but on trends that I have noticed; and because of my desire to support my love of God with an attempt to contribute to excellence in worship, these are issues about which I feel compelled to comment.

I view ministers actively involved in pastoring churches as the primary audience for this book. For them it can provide information about what parishioners think, want, and need. An important secondary audience is students preparing for the ministry. For this group, still learning the requirements of working with a congregation, the book can be a first clear look at the expectations of parishioners and can also serve as a tool for checking pastoral behavior against those expectations. Because the book is relatively short, it may be one that students-turned-pastors can keep nearby and periodically review to keep them on course in their ministry. Church leaders and officers are a tertiary audience. For example, the book is a good resource for pulpit selection committees. Understanding that effective pastors must excel at relationship building, biblical scholarship, Sunday morning exegesis presented in sermons and homilies, and everyday church administration, search committees can use the information presented in this book as an assessment tool against which pastoral candidates can be measured.

Not everyone in these anticipated audiences will agree with me about the expected role of pastors in relationship to those who sit in and learn from their pews, but my observations are an honest attempt to make a meaningful contribution to ministerial excellence by doing what I do best. I listen with a loving but critical ear, observe with a sensitive and discriminating mind, and find supportive ways to present what I have seen and heard to those I hold dear. Intended as a form of Christian service, this book illustrates the pastoral challenge of creating sermons that are intellectually stimulating, spiritually meaningful, socially relevant, and personally significant for congregants.

This book, it must be noted, is not entirely about sermons and their content. Preachers are looked upon to be pastors to their church members and to administer well the churches over which they have been given charge. This responsibility extends to behaviors that parishioners see preachers engage in from the vantage point of the pew and beyond. *View from the Pew* calls upon preachers to recognize that their behavior in and out of the pulpit influences the way that God's people hear and act on God's Word.

The chapters of *View from the Pew* address ten issues that remind preachers about the viewpoint of the parishioners and the lessons they learn from their vantage point in the service of worship. These ten points are pastoral assessment tools against which behavior can be measured in a way that provides meaningful matter for personal change and spiritual growth. Each chapter addresses an important issue in the "Preacher's Checklist" in a manner that presents a serious topic with love and occasional humor.

Throughout the book, readers should pay special attention to the information placed in notes. For flow and readability of each section, it was not always possible to include additional explanatory content within the chapter text. However, it is important to an understanding of the pew's viewpoint or, in some cases, of the author's specific viewpoint, that each note be read in context to add additional meaning to the section it supports.

Finally, each chapter ends with an attempt to balance the preacher-pew perspectives. Called "Thoughts from the Pulpit" and "Thoughts from the Pew," their descriptions are as follows:

thoughts from the pulpit

This section contains a "Preacher's Prayer," a "Pastor's Promise," and a "Minister's Message," all of which respond to the issues presented in the chapter from a pastoral perspective and state powerful objectives for addressing the concerns stated in the chapter. The three ministerial categories represent the recipient of oratorical and sermonic gifts (preacher), counseling skills and sensitivity to the human condition (pastor), and a willingness to take on the role of administrative servant to God's people (minister).

Please note: Unless context makes it appear otherwise, throughout the book the word "preacher" is used to describe the person who stands in the pulpit and gives a sermon, while "pastor" is typically reserved for that person who attends closely to the emotional needs of his or her parishioners. The roles are not mutually exclusive—a preacher can be a pastor, though a pastor is not always a preacher. As is discussed in Chapter 6: Expose the Pastor in You, there are many preachers who do not open the part of themselves that is consistently emotionally supportive and that provides their hearts to parishioners through personal time and church ministry. As in all professions there are components of a role that do not fit as nicely as we would

like or for which we are not as well suited as we would wish.
Being a pastor, a role that requires emotional compassion,
the capacity to listen, and the ability to be empathic, is not
one that all preachers can easily do. This distinction in language is therefore deliberate and hopefully provides fodder
for preacherly *and* pastoral reflection.

thoughts from the pew

This section contains a "Parishioners' Prayer" and a "Parishioners' Plea" to capture the major points addressed in the chapter from the standpoint of those who observe preachers and
participate in the shared experience of worship. Most impor-
tantly, this section is the pew's way of communicating to the
pulpit that we love and are praying with the preachers with love
to strengthen Christ's Church.

It is my prayer that preachers will find my observations useful. As a member of the Baptist church family for over thirty
years, it is my wish to make a meaningful contribution to the
discussion about the strengths and weaknesses of contempo-
rary preaching and preachers. As a keen observer of human
behavior, I hope to address pastoral behaviors that sometimes
get in God's way. By honestly addressing what parishioners
learn from the behavior and sermons of preachers, I hope to
present a challenge to preachers to provide only the best to
their parishioners, to the worthy children of God who are
eagerly awaiting God's Word.

It is hard to ignore the fact that this book is born of very
personal experiences and views. Many of the preacherly
behaviors noted herein are those that I myself have observed.

That said, I am by profession a researcher, holding a doctorate in psychology and having worked for years in the field. In this case, I have done my research, talking at great length to other pew-sitters about their observations of the pulpit and garnering from those conversations a set of principles (found in the "Preacher's Checklist" and noted as recommendations in each chapter) that reflect the observations of the collective, of "the pew." Although I am Baptist, the recommendations in *View from the Pew* are nondenominational. Other congregants with whom I discussed concerns were Protestant and Catholic, and were predominantly, though not exclusively, African American. As was my personal experience, these research subjects provided data for this book out of their love for their pastors, their respect for the sacred experience of gathering for worship, and, ultimately, their love of Christ. They join me in presenting to preachers information that can be useful to creating, through the sermonic moment and other pastoral roles and responsibilities, a space where the pulpit hears and learns from the pew.

View from the Pew represents my thoughts and prayers for the preachers with whom my life has been and continues to be blessed. This book is a gift of my heart to those who, for their love of God, preach, and whom, for their preaching, God loves.

preacher's checklist

1. Be prepared to preach.
2. Celebrate the centrality of Christ.
3. Preach God's Word, not your words.
4. Be a shepherd, not a showman.
5. Do the vision thing.
6. Expose the pastor in you.
7. Connect the head and the heart.
8. Stand on the shoulders of the saints.
9. View yourself from the pew.
10. Be satisfied.

CHAPTER 1

be prepared to preach

If you are prepared,
then you are able to feel confident.[1]

PREACHING IS, IN THE SUNDAY MORNING MOMENT, THE CENTER OF
the worship service, and as such, it is a powerful event. Because
of its centrality to the service, preaching holds great importance to its listeners. We in the pew listen carefully to preaching, take notes about what we have heard, talk about it with
our families and church friends, and buy tapes to review it in
our cars on the way to work so that the lessons of the Sunday
sermon—God's Word made flesh—can last all week. Sometimes what we learn from preaching lasts considerably longer.

I have heard a lot of excellent preaching in my life, but
interestingly, the two sermons I remember best are from my
childhood. The first, experienced when I was nine years old,
was entitled "Don't Die in Winter." Preached by Rev. Floyd
Massey, it discussed the importance of keeping your spirit
vibrant so that whenever God called you, you would be ready
to die. The sermon was peppered with stories about people
who had jeopardized their souls and traumatized their families by ignoring the beauty that God placed in their lives, by

1

refusing in the face of evident blessings to acknowledge what was good in their daily experiences. This sermon represents a seminal moment in my life. I have, since hearing it, incorporated its message fully into my approaches to social interactions, strategies for problem solving, and methods for managing crises. Every day is a marvel to me. I often have the capacity to see good where others don't. And I am a better person for the gift of that sermon in my life.

I am saved. I have believed in God all of my life as a result of the training that I received in my family and a very early awareness that the world was a magnificent creation for which a great and magnificent power must be responsible. I joined my father's church at the age of nine and was baptized by my father in a ceremony in which I became quite aware of the divine and the human acting together. I knew the import of giving my life to God, of looking at my actions and behaviors through a lens that acknowledged that I would need to account daily for my deeds. Though for years I had heard my father baptize his "brothers and sisters," on the Sunday of my baptism he acknowledged me as his "daughter"—a word that felt more beautiful at that moment than I have remembered it since. We both knew that it was special for a father to usher his daughter into a new life, having also given his daughter her first one. I was thinking these thoughts, eyes closed, feeling buoyant and protected in God's house and my father's hands. However, Daddy was also feeling something special that day, and held me under the water much longer than was safe until an observant deacon rescued my transition from sinner to a child who had chosen to walk in the light.[2]

This was not my only conversion, however; it does not represent the only or the most important moment in my soul's salvation. I hear people talk of a pivotal experience of God through which they are forever changed. Particularly striking are the stories of people whose lives have significantly changed by being born again. Though technically I am born again in the manner in which we are all reborn in Christ, I tend to view salvation differently. For me, salvation is a gradual process.[3] My salvation is a process that reflects that I am evolving in my knowledge of and relationship with God. I was saved at age nine and am saved again every day. There are chapters in my life that I recognize as places and times where God has been more present to me than was typical; these, for me, are salvation moments that take me closer to being the person God would have me become. Without exception, these salvation moments are accompanied by the memory of a sermon, well prepared and wonderfully presented.

I was baptized just after my ninth birthday. The transformation that had led to my joining the church included lots of talking with God, looking for him in unusual places, and watching him show up. "Don't Die in Winter" was evidence of the guidance for which I had prayed. As excellent sermons should do, it provided a guidepost for how to tailor my life to God's will. In much the same way that I previously had made a promise to my dentist never to eat candy, even on Halloween, I made a vow to Jesus to keep my heart in a perpetual springtime, renewed and blooming. Though in some ways this was a childlike response, it has served me well for my entire life. It is a testimony to the power of good preaching. With God's help and my fortitude, I will leave this earth in a spiritual spring.

The second life-influencing sermon, heard when I was eleven years old, was preached by Rev. Otis Moss Jr. The sermon was entitled "The Solid Rock," and its subject matter focused on the reasons why we need God. Concerned at the point that I heard this sermon that I still was not as diligent as I should be at keeping winter out of my soul, I actually rejoined the church, crying hard, deeply concerned that I had not kept my earlier promise to God. As I walked to the altar and explained that I was concerned that my baptism may not have taken and my soul may be in jeopardy, I was taken into Rev. Moss's embrace. While there, he sang, *"In times like these you need a Savior. In times like these you need an anchor. Be very sure, be very sure your anchor holds and grips the solid rock. That rock is Jesus...."* Rev. Moss's sermon and compassionate behavior taught me another important lesson: I learned that human solutions frequently fail, but Jesus never fails. It is a reminder that I have never forgotten and for which I remain grateful. Lessons learned early tend to stay with us. Traumas result from negative lessons too well learned. What a blessing that God's Word is an integral part of my earliest and most influential memories.[4]

Aside from their emotional importance in my life, these sermons had something essential in common. They were creative, well organized, scripturally sound, beautifully presented, and resonant with the lives of those who heard them. Reverends Massey and Moss were prepared to preach. Excellence for any task requires preparation. Preaching God's Word is no exception. In fact, perhaps more than in any other endeavor, those called to preach receive a tremendous challenge: to always do service to the excellent Word of God. Though we in the pew are impressed with, influenced by, and thankful for excellent preaching, we have a keen eye for bad preaching, off-days, and moments when the preacher is simply not prepared to preach.

Being prepared to preach means understanding what preaching is and should be. Preaching is:

- *An Appeal to the Community of Believers.* Preaching connects existing believers and creates new believers by naming and elucidating their shared Christian beliefs and values. Preaching aids the development and maintenance of the community of Christian believers.
- *Celebration.* Preaching celebrates the good news of Jesus and offers his salvation to anyone within its listening range. The importance of preaching as a celebratory moment is well documented. According to Rev. Dr. Frank A. Thomas, "Celebration helps the preacher motivate the people through the positive reinforcement of the gospel, which means people are motivated by the affirmative means of love, joy, hope and celebration."[5]
- *Conversation.* Preaching is a conversation with the congregation that teaches biblical history, makes references to events relevant to parishioners, and anticipates their internal (prayerful) and outward (celebratory) responses. In some traditions, such as the African American religious tradition, the sermon as conversation can take a very active form in which the preacher's exhortations are responded to in the moment with affirmations such as a hearty "Amen!" or with more direct statements that are spontaneous and individual or are part of a preacher-led "call and response" pattern.
- *An Emotional Experience.* Effective preaching creates an atmosphere charged with emotion. Through its use of imagery that can touch the hearts of listeners, preaching creates an emotional experience. Additionally, the preacher whose own passion for the preached word is evident creates an emotional environment, connecting with those in the pews in ways that create a unique shared experience. "Both theater and therapy [and preaching (my insertion)] share a common impulse—an attempt to go beyond

the everyday forms of communication to shift people's basic notion of themselves and their world. Both represent a revolt against the normal use of discourse, an understanding of the natural limits of rhetoric and recognition that *communication is at least as much an emotional phenomenon as a linguistic one.*"[6]

- *Exhortation.* "Exhortation," defined as "something designed to urge or persuade" or "the giving of advice,"[7] in the context of a sermon persuades listeners about the liberating qualities of salvation and advises them regarding strategies for living Godly lives.

- *An Invocation of the Holy Spirit.* The preaching moment cannot happen without a direct invocation of the God of history who stood with his people, leading them through the actual and spiritual wilderness, and the God who even today brings us through difficult and triumphant times. Though the Holy Spirit is ever-present, preaching invokes that presence aloud and welcomes it into the community of believers.

- *An Opportunity for Biblical Exegesis.* The sermonic moment is one in which the preacher uses Scripture to make specific points that will bring meaning and richness to those in the pews. As "exegesis,"[8] preaching teaches by explaining and interpreting biblical texts.

- *A Spiritual Gift.* Preaching, particularly excellent preaching, can be seen as, and is, a unique gift from God. After all, the call to the ministry is a sign that God has placed his hand on the preacher, guiding that person in the development of spiritual gifts that he or she contributes to God's people through preaching. In this sense, preaching highlights the preacher's God-given oratorical gifts and can also be a gift to the life and spirit of the hearer.

With these definitions in mind, and aware that sermons can be powerful tools for personal change among those who hear them, the well-prepared preacher has several important challenges, some of which will be addressed in the remainder of this chapter.

show yourself approved unto god
"Study to show thyself approved unto God."
(2 Timothy 2:15)

A heart that loves and honors God is essential to the work of the ministry, but it is not enough. Preachers must study God's Word to understand it as a tool for furthering his kingdom, to learn his purpose in their own lives, to understand the direction that they must take their congregations to enlarge the church of God, and to adequately teach it to church members.

To do this requires understanding that education and the avenues it provides for self-improvement are gifts from God. This, however, is a particular challenge in an increasing national climate of anti-intellectualism and conservatism that has emerged in some of our churches. Conservatism is not defined here in political terms but as increasingly fundamentally narrow scriptural interpretations, more autocratic pastor-parishioner relationships, and the tendency for those of us in the pews to feel that our questions about theology and what is required to be children of God are unwelcome.[9]

Historic church weaknesses, such as anti-intellectualism, must be aggressively addressed by church leaders committed to the growth of Christ's kingdom.[10] More than anything, anti-intellectualism represents insecurity on the part of those church leaders who fear that highly educated parishioners are likely to question pastoral teachings. God does not want us to forget that African Americans fought for educational opportunity, and we should respect and nurture God's gift of intelligence to us.[11] Preparation and trust in God is the antidote to anti-intellectualism.

Preachers whom I have known tend to have two days of the week set aside for sermon preparation: one dedicated to study of the selected text, and another set aside for writing the sermon. This type of deliberate preparation is highly likely to result in a sermon that finds a spot in the heart of parishioners. We know when sermons have been well prepared and when they have been slapped together. We also know when the preacher has studied the text and found meaning in it that, more than just teaching the parishioners, holds personal meaning for them.

Parishioners do not assume that preachers ever take the Word of God lightly. However, just as a poorly prepared physician imperils patients, a poorly prepared preacher confuses spirits and imperils souls. For the preacher, showing oneself "approved unto God" means making certain that the preparation of the sermon is as important as the placement of it in the worship service.

learn the news on preaching

"It is no use walking anywhere to preach unless our walking is our preaching."[12]

Another component of personal training for the ministry and of being prepared to preach is understanding the purpose of preaching. The preceding quotation is quite serious in its teaching intent. Walking one's preaching means, above all else, taking responsibility for the content of one's sermons, understanding that parishioners come to church to be fed God's Word. God's Word, then, must be well interpreted and responsibly presented by the preacher. To reach those in the pews in a meaningful way, sermons must contain a combination of expert exegesis, emotional content, and relevant connection to the issues that church members bring through the church doors. In recent years there has been some concern that a lack of seminary training (or other training that provides ministers with a deep understanding of biblical texts) has created "Sermon Lite." Additionally, the access to free or purchasable sermons on the Internet has created the opportunity for some preachers to "cheat."

Recently, these issues were addressed in a newspaper article by Dean Smith entitled "An Era When the Art of the Sermon Has Declined."[13] The article discussed the significant concern that too many preachers no longer have the skills required to be "great" preachers. Noting that fewer preachers have broad-based liberal arts educations than in previous years, that ministry is increasingly a second career, and that sermons on many topics can be easily downloaded from the Internet (increasing opportunities for plagiarism at worst and unoriginal efforts at best), Smith and those whom he interviewed feared the "deterioration of the sermon as a literary craft or, some would say, an art form."[14]

According to Smith, this concern is not unfounded. In the past few years, several legal cases have arisen from preachers plagiarizing the words of other preachers. Smith notes that although many preachers don't trust their own capacity to craft sermons that will be interesting to their congregations, this worry is rarely justified, because personal experience allows preachers to find in their own relationship with God something that will be meaningful to their parishioners. "That's what a good talker can do," one source was quoted as saying. "Poke down and give voice to something that may seem incoherent but, once it's out in the open, people can hang their lives on it and say, 'Yes, there's hope, there's meaning.'"

Excellent theological and homiletics training, whether for first- or second-career ministers, is a simple way to ensure that the craft and art of preaching remain alive. Being prepared to preach also requires that one's walking shows up in one's preaching.

be a seminarian

And be not conformed to this world: but be ye transformed by the renewing of your mind, that ye may prove what is that good, and acceptable, and perfect, will of God. (Romans 12:2)

Preparation, for preaching or any other task, is first and foremost an educational process. Education is essential for personal development and for the perpetuation of our culture as strong and capable of growth in the new century. In every avenue of American industry we often bemoan the fact that there are too few well-prepared workers. We express dismay that our universities are filled with students who don't reason well or write proficiently. We are concerned that even in the most low-level jobs, people don't possess the requisite skills for success. We should have these exact same concerns about the ministry, about an arena of work in which God is to be glorified and through which new souls are to be brought to Christ.

Some preachers believe that being touched by the hand of God is sufficient preparation for the pulpit. On Tavis Smiley's recent C-SPAN forum on the State of the Black Church, Rev.

Dr. Jeremiah A. Wright Jr., of Chicago's Trinity United Church of Christ, explained that doctors have to go to medical school to become doctors and lawyers have to attend law school to become lawyers; ministers must do the same (my paraphrase). This form of preparation is an excellent first step toward showing oneself approved unto God.

Designed for this purpose, seminaries provide rich opportunities to study God's Word, to learn about God and Jesus Christ through deliberate historical exploration of biblical and other sacred texts. Such training enables the preacher to share accurate information with parishioners, information that greatly facilitates the parishioners' own Bible study and walk with God.

Once preachers are prepared through deliberate study, their sermons are wonderful opportunities to teach parishioners about the history and traditions of the Bible and to use its lessons to explain current social issues or to make connections to the personal life concerns of parishioners. Being prepared to preach means that the preacher must have done more than just memorize Bible verses. He or she must understand the Bible's broader context and place the selected text in context for the people of God. In order to teach God's Word through preaching, preachers must know the Word, understand the history of the Word within its social and political contexts, and communicate it effectively to a congregation that lives in the here and now. To be an undereducated preacher teaches those in the pews that the gift of schooling provided for us by God is not valued, that the Christian education that could be provided to us is not thought to be essential, and that the preacher does not consider it important to engage in personal Christian learning as a lifelong activity.

organize for excellence

"Every sermon must make sense; it must be manifestly reasonable and generally consistent with an orderly understanding of God's creation and our experience in it.... Therefore, when one has arrived at an acceptably cogent flow chart or outline of sermon ideas, one has only begun the preparation by ensuring that its very flow will not be an intellectual obstacle."[15]

If preaching requires preparation, how might preachers prepare? In addition to assuring that one has received an appropriate pastoral education through seminary training, Rev. Dr. Frank A. Thomas suggests use of tools such as a "Preaching Worksheet." This tool focuses on the organization required to prepare the sermon. It helps preachers organize the preaching moment by asking them to honestly consider the following questions:

- What does this passage of Scripture say to me?
- What does this passage say to the needs of people in our time?
- What is the "bad news" in the text? What is the "bad news" for our time?
- What is the "good news" in the text? What is the "good news" for our time?
- What is the behavioral purpose of this sermon? What illustrations will meaningfully address critical needs in the congregation and describe the "means through which God will deliver the community from its problems and despair"?[16]
- What and how shall we celebrate?[17]

As a way of organizing for excellence, these and other questions are useful sermon preparation tools. It is important for the preacher to understand that the pew expects excellence and organization from the pulpit. These days, parishioners come to church with notebooks, taking notes on the exact Scripture and points of the sermon. Many churches also provide sermons on audiocassette or videotape immediately after the service. With plans to study the text and sermon during the week, parishioners soon discover if the sermon was sloppily constructed.

William C. Turner Jr. asks his student preachers to regard preparation to preach as understanding the mystery. The mystery is the God-moment in which God speaks truth to you and you know that the voice with which you will speak to your congregation is real, valid, and Spirit-filled. There are many times, however, when lack of preparation shows itself to the pew as well, with evidence that the preacher and mystery did not meet each other on a particular Sunday morning.

> [B]eing prepared to preach requires touching the mystery that is not accessible on the preacher's terms. Great risk is involved in presuming to set the time when the mystery can be touched. More time may be required by the mystery than has been allotted. If one makes the approach too late, there may not be time to listen, to receive, to be formed. This is the problem of preaching a draft that is awful, being caught in a bind that affords no alternative. When the mystery has not been touched, there is no vitality, no power. Preaching that does not live cannot give life; preaching that has no power cannot give power.[18]

It insults God and the congregation when the preacher enters the pulpit unprepared or when the sermon is poorly organized or shoddily presented. Presiding over the service of worship is an honor and a responsibility. As a part of worship, preaching is an exquisitely important act. Like presiding over worship, or perhaps even more so, preaching is a high honor and an exceptional responsibility. Excellent preaching is the result of a prepared heart. It flows well, like the rhythm of a well-constructed story. It should present a scriptural text, create in its hearers increased understanding of God's Word and capacity for life-changing actions based on that Word, invoke the presence of the Holy Spirit, and provide an opportunity for shared corporate celebration. Every sermon should have the potential to be for its hearers what "Don't Die in Winter" and "The Solid Rock" were for me.

learn the notes, *then* improvise
"Excellence takes practice."[19]

Excellence requires organization, but it also takes practice. One of my friends, a young minister with an amazing life and story and an elegance and eloquence of language, could easily hold people in rapt attention from the pulpit through the spontaneous weaving of stories and Scripture. He never allows himself the easy indulgence of spontaneity, though. Saturday mornings tend to find him unavailable for get-togethers with friends because he is more likely to be walking around his living room practicing his sermon aloud. Because he knows that he has the "gift of gab," he does not want ever to be accidentally glib in the pulpit. So he practices his sermons, understanding that his natural gifts for oratory will allow him to check in with the Holy Spirit during the delivery of the sermon and determine if some of his life's stories can add meaningfully to the worship experience. My friend understands the importance of practice in the preaching moment.

The Spirit indeed moves in mysterious and spontaneous ways in the preaching moment through preachers. Improvisation can be good, but some preachers spend so much time improvising that the pew doesn't know what you are preaching about. Sermons must have meaning, content, context, texture, and a readily definable beginning, middle, and end. If in that sequence, the preacher, like a good musician, feels the Spirit and takes off on a "riff," that interlude will enrich the preaching and help the souls of the listeners in the pew. But too often those riffs last too long, or appear, unwittingly, to be inhabited by the spirit, not of Christ, but of someone's dear relative— the one who tells the stories at the dinner table that everyone dreads because they go on too long and after a while no one knows the point. That relative should never be the spirit of improvisation that inhabits one's sermon. Unfortunately, that spirit shows up, all over America, in the pulpit, on many a Sunday morning.

A recent movie provided an unexpected opportunity to be reminded that the old adage "Practice makes perfect" is true. *Drumline* tells the story of two bands that take part in the annual band competition that is important on the campuses of historically black colleges. A young man who is a born talent as a drummer is unable to read music, which is a requirement for the school for whose band he is training. He finds this to be a ridiculous rule; after all, he can observe others, listen to their rhythms, imitate them exactly, and then add his own improvisational twists. The problem that he does not recognize is that there is a limit to everyone's talent, particularly when they don't have at their disposal the tools required to help them get all they can from the talents with which they have been blessed. He had good reason for this confusion: the band that always wins the band competition doesn't care whether its band members can read music or not. His band, which always loses, pays almost too much attention to its training needs. The bands finally face off and find themselves in a tie, a tie that is won by the better-trained band.

Why is the lesson of this movie important to preachers? Preachers often have special oratorical gifts. However, if they are not truly prepared to preach (by seminary training, mentoring processes, and practice), they will at some point find themselves at a loss in their pulpits, unable to teach the lessons of the Bible because they have no answers to the theological questions raised by what they preach.

As a final illustration for this point, I present one learned by my grandfather, a minister for forty years, that was taught to my father, who at this point in his career has been a minister for more than fifty. Here are the words of my paternal grandfather, Rev. Dr. Wade Hampton McKinney II:

> While helping my father plow the land we were sharecropping in Northeast Georgia, he told me to bring the wagon from under the tree out to where he was working in the field. This was my first chance to drive the team of mules. No sooner was I in the driver's seat than the mules bolted. The wagon overturned. My father pulled me from under the wagon and said, "I should whip you, but you've been whipped enough." The wagon was loaded with manure. Then he gave me some advice which has stood me in good stead down through the years. "The next time you drive anything, take the reins before you grab the whip."[20]

As a final recommendation, I encourage preachers to learn the lessons of *Drumline;* of my friend who practices his sermons on Saturdays; and of my grandfather, who learned the importance of taking the reins before grabbing the whip. In other words, learn the notes, preacher, *then* improvise.

preach the word, preach the word, preach the word
*"Education is not the filling of a pail,
but the lighting of a fire."*[21]

Once the notes have been learned, improvisation is a privilege
of preaching, allowing preachers to, in the lines of an old
gospel tune, *"Preach the Word, preach the Word, preach the
Word! (If I never, ever see you any more, I will meet you on
the other shore.)"* Preaching is, in some ways, the performed
Word of God. It is an opportunity for the preacher to demonstrate the fruits of time spent in digging into the mine of the
Scripture in search of ideas, specific biblical history, and tex-
tual relevance to the lives of those sitting in the pews. As the
primary format for Christian education,[22] preaching in the
Sunday morning context is the main way that many parishioners learn about the Bible.

For those of us in the pew, preaching is also the scriptural
education that fills the empty space in our lives, answers questions important to our daily living, and lights spiritual fires
within us. When preachers preach the Word, parishioners
learn and are edified. As a tool for changing lives, preaching
(that results from the "POP" process: preparation, organization, practice) meets parishioners where they are and has the
capacity to move them to where their souls need to be.

I believe, however, that preaching has this power only when
it is comprised of a specific interaction between the pulpit and
the pew. Sometimes this is subtle—a quiet acceptance of what
has been said, seen perhaps in a thoughtful nodding of heads.
Other times it is more vocal. In all cases, it has the components of the "call and response" tradition—the preacher calls
through questions or statements directed to the people in the
pews, and they spontaneously respond.

The Call. How the pew responds to the call often has to do with the relationship between the pew and the pulpit (or the pulpit and the pew). The call, in this sense, also has a lot to do with the parishioners' expectation of the preacher. I have been accused of speaking *ex cathedra* (speaking for God by virtue of one's office) from time to time; my pastor, Dr. H. Beecher Hicks, and I have laughingly discussed the conversation that I will need to have with Jesus one day to explain my occasional tendency to put words in his mouth. I know without a doubt that I cannot speak for God. However, I think it fair to say also that God has high expectations of preachers, of those who, in the depths of their own souls, have heard and responded to his voice in a very particular way. In that sense, the call is about the preacher who has been called to preach in a sacred conversation with the Lord. Calls to the ministry are between the called and the Lord. Trusting those calls, parishioners open themselves to the Word that channels from the ultimate source through the preacher. The preachers' words, therefore, are more than words and should be highly regarded for the power that others attach to them.

The Response. Parishioners share high expectations of those who stand in the pulpit and interpret God's Word. Building the kingdom of God is an enormous responsibility and an essential pastoral duty. We parishioners notice "preacher-fire." We are moved when we see it, listen carefully when we hear it, and often are pushed to action by it. According to Rev. Henry H. Mitchell, "The hearers are always the actors. The desired behavior may be for them to grow in forgiveness, honesty, unselfish service, or commitment to labor for peace or against world hunger."[23] Powerful, strategic, and thoughtful preaching clears the path and shows us the way to Christ's robe and God's throne. And those in the pews respond powerfully to the power of Christ that is evident when the one in the pulpit evidences God's call by truly preaching the Word.

thoughts from the pulpit

Preacher's Prayer: O Lord, teach me the precious intricacies of your Word. Give me patience to learn it, the wisdom to understand it, and the fortitude to distill it for your people. Let me stand in your presence as an open vessel through which your Word can flow. Amen.

Pastor's Promise: I will seek to honor God's Word by adequately preparing myself to preach it to his people. I will study it in its multiple historical contexts, interpret it from its theological and denominational perspectives, and prayerfully communicate it to my church members.

Minister's Message: I will engage in the "POP" process, undertaking the preparation, organization, and practice required for excellence in preaching. I will make time in my schedule for biblical study and weekly sermon preparation, and I will teach the importance of preparation for the preaching moment to those whom I train. Preparation to preach will be evident in me.

thoughts from the pew

Parishioners' Prayer: Dear Lord, open our ears to the hearing of your Word, so excellently prepared by our pastor. Open our eyes to opportunities for service to you. Open our hearts so that we might demonstrate through our actions a willingness to live for you. Let us hear and respond. Amen.

Parishioners' Plea: Dear Pastor, as you prepare yourself to preach, prepare us, through the design and intent of your sermons, to better understand Christ and to serve him in the world, but first in our hearts.

NOTES

1. Robert J. Ringer, http://www.quotationspage.com (accessed September 14, 2002).

2. The subtle joke here is that my father got "happy" while he as baptizing me, and in so doing, almost drowned me! He almost purified my soul and sent me to heaven in one fell swoop!

3. I should explain that I do not think of conversion in the way that most people do. As I explain in my book *Christian Education in the African American Church,* while I believe that there is clearly a moment at which God comes into our lives and we become aware of God's significance to us, I think that if we keep our spirits open to God, we are saved and are being saved in every moment of our lives.

4. All those with whom I have spoken likewise had clear memories of sermons that were particularly important to them. Here, I chose to relate my own experiences because they were the clearest examples of sermons heard young that have lifelong impact.

5. Frank A. Thomas, *They Like to Never Quit Praisin' God: The Role of Celebration in Preaching* (Cleveland: United Church Press, 1997), 45.

6. Edwin H. Friedman, "Theater and Therapy," *The Family Therapy Networker* 8, no. 1 (January–February 1984), as quoted in Frank A. Thomas, *They Like to Never Quit Praisin' God: The Role of Celebration in Preaching* (Cleveland, United Church Press, 1997), 4.

7. Keyword "exhortation," http://encarta.msn.com (accessed March 18, 2003).

8. Keyword "exegesis," http://encarta.msn.com (accessed March 18, 2003). This term, from the Greek word meaning "to guide," is the

explanation or interpretation of texts, especially those from the Bible.

9. In *Christian Education in the African American Church: A Guide for Teaching Truth,* I cite numerous stories, as examples of what constitutes poor teaching, that are also indicators of the ways that this form of conservatism has seeped into our churches. Additionally, from the standpoint of the pew, there are increasing numbers of us who are coming to the church wanting an easy path to heaven and, in this sense, are often not asking the tough questions.

10. See Lora-Ellen McKinney, *Total Praise: An Orientation to Black Baptist Belief and Worship* (Valley Forge, Pa.: Judson Press, 2003), 84.

11. Ibid., 86.

12. St. Francis of Assisi, http://www.quotationspage.com (accessed September 14, 2002).

13. Dean Smith, "An Era When the Art of the Sermon Has Declined," Religion Journal, *New York Times,* March 30, 2002, sec. B, p. 6, col. 1.

14. Ibid.

15. Henry H. Mitchell, *Celebration and Experience in Preaching* (Nashville: Abingdon Press, 1990), 21–22.

16. Thomas, *They Like to Never Quit Praisin' God,* 115.

17. Ibid., 75, 114–15.

18. William C. Turner Jr., "From Scribble to Script: Preparing to Preach," *The African American Pulpit,* Winter 2003–2004, Vol. 7, No.1, 22.

19. Louise Jones McKinney (the author's mother).

20. Wade Hampton McKinney II, former pastor of Antioch Baptist Church, Cleveland, Ohio, November 1954. Quoted in Floyd Massey and Samuel McKinney, *Church Administration in the Black Perspective* (Valley Forge, Pa.: Judson Press, 2003), 26.

21. W. B. Yeats, http://www.quotationspage.com (accessed July 27, 2002).

22. See Lora-Ellen McKinney, *Christian Education in the African American Church: A Guide for Teaching Truth* (Valley Forge, Pa.: Judson Press, 2003), sec. 3.

23. Mitchell, *Celebration and Experience,* 53.

CHAPTER 2

celebrate
the centrality of christ

Is your all on the altar of sacrifice laid?
Your heart does the Spirit control?
You can only be blest,
And have peace and sweet rest,
As you yield Him your body and soul.[1]

I AM FASCINATED BY CHURCH ARCHITECTURE FOR ONE QUITE SIMPLE reason. In the modern world, it remains the only form of architecture to have meaning beyond its pure function and form. In an age of ego, and particularly of pastoral ego, church architecture holds, I believe, important lessons for preachers about who they are in relation to both God and humankind. Let me explain this through a personal example.

Though not a part of my Baptist tradition, the experience of being in a cathedral is one that I greatly enjoy. For centuries, cathedral floor plans have been constructed with a central nave and a broad passage before the pulpit to deliberately reproduce the cross as essential to their design. I love knowing that when I stand in its center, I am literally *in* the cross. I am also filled with awe at the size of cathedrals, at their large arching ceilings that have a dual purpose: to reach toward the heavens and to reinforce the smallness of humankind in relation to the vastness of the universe and the majesty and glory of God, its Creator.

Because of this fascination with church architecture and what it teaches about people and their beliefs, I visit houses of worship everywhere I travel. On a recent church trip to the Bahamas, I visited a church that has a prayer grotto built into an ancient stone wall. The wall was designed to replicate the Western Wall in Jerusalem, and supplicants can circle it in prayer, take walks in a prayer courtyard, or enter a prayer center where, in private booths, they can call on God for themselves or for others. This space is open twenty-four hours a day and is filled with those wishing to deepen their relationships with God or seeking support for specific issues or needs in their lives. Involved in a building campaign, this congregation plans to build its new sanctuary above the stone wall of the grotto. Their building plans teach a clear lesson. This church has made it evident from theological, behavioral, and architectural perspectives that the foundation of their belief is prayer.

The importance of church architecture to the experience of worship is as old as the building of the ancient Israelite tabernacle. Martin Luther, for example, the father of the Protestant Reformation, understood early the religious symbolism of architecture. In stark contrast to the design of Catholic pulpits placed on the side of the church sanctuary (often with stairs that elevated the priests to a position of power by symbolically placing them above the heads of the congregation), Luther wanted Protestant church design to reflect its revolutionary theology. His theological treatises strongly stated that believers could speak to God for themselves, not requiring priests as intermediaries. As a result, Protestant churches typically have lower ceilings—an architectural representation of God's direct accessibility to the average person. Worried that parishioners ascribed to their pastors characteristics that should be attributed to God only, Luther also moved the pulpit to the center of the church as an illustration that Christ alone was central to the process of worship and the lives of believers.

This, then, is the important point of this brief lesson in architecture. A central complaint of church members interviewed for this book is that pastoral egos have run amok. Pastors, they worry, have forgotten that Christ, not the pastor, is central to the experience of worship. For long-time members, this creates anger and confusion, occasionally resulting in an exodus of established members, or in other cases causing diminished tithes and offerings. In new members, it creates a warped perception of who the preacher is and what his or her role must be.

When doing Christian education workshops on Baptist polity, I always ask church members who is the head of the church and they invariably respond, "The pastor." In Baptist church government, which is *democratic and congregational, Christ* is the head of the church, followed by the congregation and then the pastor and other church officers. That Christ heads the church should be a no-brainer. The pastor is indeed powerful, but in the Baptist model, the pastor is elected by the congregation. In Methodist, Episcopal, Catholic, and other traditions, pastors are assigned to congregations. Christ heads the church in all cases! The preacher-pastor-minister is the undershepherd of Christ.

Preachers must remember that although they have roles important to the building of God's kingdom, they themselves are not central to worship.[2] One of my best friends called me recently about an experience at her church. It was the morning when the choir anniversary was to be celebrated, a time of thanking the choir members for their service. As was planned for this annual event, my friend and her choir sang more than the normal complement of songs, and for their efforts they received a warm and wonderful response from the congregation. Because music that honors God is, of itself, a ministry, some pastors might have kept their comments short, simply expressing thanks that the church choir so honored God through music. Other pastors might have preached, but limited the length of the sermon because the choir had, in this instance, brought God's Word to the people through song. Instead, my friend's minister stood up and stated that no one came to church to hear the choir. They came, he said, to hear the preacher. He then preached for an inappropriately long time and sang *twelve* songs himself. The choir felt hurt, the congregation was confused, and the minister clearly had no idea of the many ways that he had dishonored the pulpit, the pew, and himself.

He and other preachers with such inclinations need to remember this: it's not about the preacher, nor is it about the pew—it's about the Lamb of God. *"Only Thou art holy; there is none beside Thee, Perfect in pow'r, in love, and purity."*[3] Christ alone is central. This crucial fact is far too often forgotten.

don't limit the size of god's house
The Church of God is people.

As described above, a component of maintaining the centrality of Christ is an understanding of the role of the preacher as being a conduit for God's Word rather than a special vessel of God who speaks *ex cathedra.*[4] Those in the pew do not doubt

25

that the preacher has been called by God to serve in the church; rather, they ask the preacher to respect that the experience of worship should have as one of its aims the pure divination of God's Word, unsullied, as much as is possible, by human actions.

Another way to understand Christ as being central is for the pulpit to communicate to the pew an understanding that God is everywhere. The church is the house of God, but it is not the only place where God resides. It is essential for parishioners to understand that God lives in their hearts and in the world. It is important that parishioners not spend all of their time in the church building as part of an insurance plan for making it to heaven. Preachers must teach parishioners the vastness of God's reach and the expanse of his presence. In practical terms this means:

- Encouraging parishioners to be good stewards of their time and resources, spending sufficient time with their families and on the duties required by their jobs.
- Not expecting parishioners to spend all of their spare time at the church, because if God is in our hearts, then ministry can happen anywhere.
- Encouraging parishioners to be well organized, spending time at the church for scheduled ministries, Bible study, worship, and activities for which they hold specific responsibilities.
- Facilitating family-focused ministries.
- Encouraging community volunteer work.
- Demonstrating respect for the pulpit and the pew by behaving honorably.

This viewpoint, stated from the pulpit, demonstrated through the actions of church leaders, or taught in Christian education classes as part of responsible stewardship, respects the centrality of Christ. It understands that it is important not to limit the size of God's house by expecting all of his work to be done inside the walls of the church.

journey to the center of the soul
Jesus is all the world to me, My life, my joy, my all.[5]

Pastoral understanding of the centrality of Christ and the capacity to teach it to those in the pews both require a bit of soul-searching. Perhaps an earth-bound story can serve as a metaphor for this idea. Praised for its vision of the world and its literary style, Jules Verne's nineteenth-century masterpiece, *Journey to the Center of the Earth,* placed Professor Lieden-brock and his nephew Axel in a journey across the vast expanse of Iceland and into a crater in the sea, where they confront humankind's early history. As a story, it relates a remarkable adventure. As a perspective, it explores conflicting views of human origins. As a psychological treatise, it por-trays the journey as a feature of travel that is as important, or more important, than reaching the destination.

If this story is seen as a metaphor for preaching, then there is much that a preacher can learn from it. When blended with good pastoring, good preaching helps parishioners along their soul's journey, an essential process whose intermittent (with fits and starts) and final destination are the same. With the help of those who shepherd them, Christians journey toward Christ. And anyone who would shepherd others towards Christ, which is the pastor's role, must likewise be on a spiritual journey. In much the same way that we cite the maxim "Physician, heal thyself," we call upon the preacher to know not only God, but also himself or herself in relationship to God.

A praise song sung in our churches says, *"The Jesus in me loves the Jesus in you."* When Christ is the destination of the preacher's journey, and when the preacher encourages this difficult but rewarding journey for those in the pew, they see it, recognize it, and appreciate it.

preach to the coasts
"Human beings have (1) a basic need for identity and authenticity, and (2) a basic need to move into relationship with others."[6]

An important component of celebrating the centrality of Christ, and of letting the Jesus in the pulpit truly love the Jesus in the pew (and vice versa), requires a focus on the pew that deals with us from a place of equality. Rev. Dr. Gardner C. Taylor referred to this as "being a person from their own coasts." This self-explanatory statement is a reminder that though God has placed a special call on the life of the preacher, the preacher is a person as are we and should see in us our humanity and deal with us from a level place. When we are preached to as if the preacher recognizes us, we respond in a much different, stronger, and more personal way to the Word of God. Preach to the coasts, preacher, and we will swim out to meet you every time.

let christ be your all in all
He is my strength from day to day, Without Him I would fall.[7]

You who are preachers show us in the pew, through your words and actions, on whom it is that your lives are focused. We recognize Jesus in you. And if the devil is there, we will recognize him also. As a model for us, behave well. Show respect for your job and its position of influence in your and our lives and in the life of the larger community by carefully choosing your words, by participating in the issues that impact the church and the community outside the church (don't limit the size of God's house!), and by being respectful to those with whom you come into contact. Show respect for us by being interested in our lives, valuing our time, and giving evidence through preaching and other behaviors that Christ lives in you. Show the centrality of Christ in your life, and by doing so, guide us to closer walks with Christ.

thoughts from the pulpit

Preacher's Prayer: Heavenly Father, though I may be tempted by the elevation of my office to consider myself therefore elevated, remind me that I am your child. I am not larger than you. I am not better than my parishioners. Though skilled I may be, I am not a star among preachers, using my pulpit as a place to show my preacherly prowess and verbal might. With you in my sight and your love in my heart, I ask that you grant me the strength to keep you in the center of my life. Amen.

Pastor's Promise: I will seek to keep worship services focused on their sole purpose, which is to glorify God. I will ask God's presence in the center of my soul and the core of my being. Let it show.

Minister's Message: I will work with the officers of the church, the department of Christian education, and all ministers on staff to develop missions, ministries, programs, and processes that are Christ-centered, God-focused, theologically correct, and socially relevant. I will engage with my church members in ways that teach that Christ is central and that our task is to work collectively as the body of Christ, creating a strong church and community that brings honor to God.

thoughts from the pew

Parishioners' Prayer: Dear Lord, we ask that you reside in our hearts and our spirits. We pray that you be with us in our every thought and act. We vow to make you the center of our joy.

Parishioners' Plea: Dear Pastor, we pledge you our support and prayers, though not our adulation. We pray into your life, as we seek in our own, the continued capacity to be humble servants of Christ.

NOTES

1. Elisha A. Hoffman, "Is Your All on the Altar" in *African American Heritage Hymnal,* ed. Delores Carpenter and Nolan E. Williams Jr. (Chicago: GIA Publications, 2001), 393. Copyright © by GIA Publications, Inc., Chicago, Illinois. All rights reserved. Used with permission.

2. Don't misunderstand. Preachers are important to worship. They organize it, preach in it, and guide parishioners through it. But *Christ* alone is *central* to it.

3. Reginald Heber, "Holy, Holy, Holy! Lord God Almighty," in *African American Heritage Hymnal,* ed. Delores Carpenter and Nolan E. Williams Jr. (Chicago: GIA Publications, 2001), 329. Copyright © by GIA Publications, Inc., Chicago, Illinois. All rights reserved. Used with permission.

4. To speak "ex cathedra" means speaking for God by virtue of one's office. The Roman Catholic faith believes that the Pope is commissioned by God to speak; this is not a belief of Protestants. My observations in this regard are directed at Protestant ministers.

5. Will L. Thompson, "Jesus Is All the World to Me," in *African American Heritage Hymnal,* ed. Delores Carpenter and Nolan E.

Williams Jr. (Chicago: GIA Publications, 2001), 382. Copyright ©
by GIA Publications, Inc., Chicago, Illinois. All rights reserved.
Used with permission.

6.   Frank A. Thomas. *They Like to Never Quit Praisin' God: The
     Role of Celebration in Preaching* (Cleveland: United Church Press,
     1997), 13.

7.   Will L. Thompson, "Jesus Is All the World to Me," 382.

preach god's word, not your words

Is there a Word from the Lord?
Send your Word. Send your Word.
Your Word can save sinners,
Reclaim backsliders,
Encourage believers,
Send your Word.[1]

PREACHING, THE CENTRAL COMPONENT OF MANY CHRISTIAN worship services,[2] is part of an order of worship, all of whose elements are designed to invoke the presence of God, clarify the questions of believers and nonbelievers, provide an experience of worship and congregational communion, and bring souls to Christ. For those in the pew, the sermon is a moment of worship—personally relevant, hopefully meaningful, and potentially life-changing—that occurs in the presence of a corporate body of believers. For the preacher, the sermon is, of itself, a rite; it represents a passage and responsibility for which he or she has trained and has innate or developed skills, and for which, if the truth be told, there is bit of competition among those verbally gifted in delivering the Word of God. Finally, the sermon is a component of a larger rite (the service of worship, including Scripture, music, tithes and offerings, and individual and corporate prayer), and it serves as a grounding celebratory ritual for congregants.

don't exalt the preacher
God resisteth the proud, but giveth grace unto the humble. (James 4:6)

The preacher is, without a doubt, quite important to the service of worship. However, no matter how gifted the preacher is in sermonic delivery, the service is always about what happens when people come together to worship God as "one body in Christ."

Even though the 1980s (the "Me Generation") taught a very different lesson, the truth is that worship and preaching are really not about "me." Preaching is about the Father, the Son, and the Holy Ghost. Amen and amen.

work out your personal issues in therapy
The good news of the Gospel is that there is a resource of divine mercy which is able to overcome a contradiction within our own souls, which we cannot ourselves overcome.[3]

In this day and age, when so little is sacred, the church is our sacred gathering space, and the pulpit is its Holy of Holies. Thus, it is essential that the pulpit be respected and not be used for purposes that are "personal" to the preacher or that might in any other way sully the sanctity of the space. Among the things that can sully the pulpit are preachers who bring to their sermons the wrong spirit, including the tendency to speak one's own words rather than those of the Lord, Christ Jesus.

Here is an illustrative example. I have been in the church of a preacher who possesses considerable oratorical skills. However, a large portion of his congregation appears to be confused about the topic of his sermons on any given Sunday. His sermons, though well organized, always seem overly personal and somewhat negative. He uses the Scriptures to berate whoever made him angry during the week. The sermons' references might well be lost upon anyone who is unaware of church gossip. This is an inappropriate use of the pulpit. On certain occasions, systemic issues that require the attention of the church perhaps should be addressed from the pulpit. However, issues with particular parishioners or church committees should be taken care of in meetings. Sustained anger on the part of the preacher and issues of chronic conflict avoidance with specific parishioners or church groups require personal prayer and therapeutic intervention. Preachers, please don't work out your dysfunctions on us in the pews. We have enough problems of our own. And certainly, don't do it from the pulpit.

A childhood memory of mine illustrates a related point. In children's church one Sunday, we were told by a minister-in-training that God kept the names of naughty children in his "Big Black Book." If we were not sufficiently repentant, God would descend from heaven with his holy whip and tan our terrible hides. Some of us, though disturbed by this news, understood somehow that it was merely sanctified silliness. Other children were truly terrified. This teaching was more than silly, however. It was untrue and unfair. It was theologically false and ran the risk of poisoning impressionable minds and turning them away from Christ or causing them to believe for the wrong reasons.

These examples serve to make a very important point: preachers should not use the pulpit as their personal bully platforms. Preachers who do so cheapen worship, teach improper lessons to the members who sit in the pews, discourage potential believers whose very souls have been placed in their presence for a special purpose, and insult the sacred nature of the altar that they have been called to exalt. Preacher, preach God's Word, not your words. And work out your personal issues in therapy.

don't exalt the pew

For do I now persuade men, or God? or do I seek to please men? for if I yet pleased men, I should not be the servant of Christ. (Galatians 1:10)

Just as the preacher is not to be exalted, preaching God's Word also means keeping all components of the church and its people in perspective. The pew is to be respected, but not exalted. All of us (both preachers and church members) have been in the congregations of preachers who seem to pay extra-special attention to parishioners who have fame or the good fortune of finances that can benefit the church. Though such members have access to things that can benefit the church and its programs and certainly should be asked to use their resources to support the work of the church, they, as persons, are no more special than anyone else. Preachers may praise their efforts, but they should not elevate them to sainthood. Remember also the story of the widow's mite (Mark 12:41-44). All who provide from God's goodness to them should be given credit for their contributions. But that praise must be done in

35

a way that values the work and honors the worker without exalting them. God alone is to be lifted up. The church should celebrate the contributions of the pastor, the accomplishments of its members, and the success of its ministries, always remembering that all are working to honor Christ through their activities.

respect pew time

Time is filled with swift transitions;
Naught of earth unmoved can stand.
Build your hopes on things eternal;
Hold to God's unchanging hand.[4]

Part of the contract between the pulpit and the pew is related to how the two groups that they represent relate over the issue of time. Because of the importance of the sermon to the completeness of the worship experience, many preachers tend to take too much time to deliver their messages. This, too, can be tied up in pastoral ego. Although the preacher may, in fact, be speaking God's Word beautifully (as opposed to his or her own in the guise of God's), observing the sanctity of the pulpit also means using the pew's time wisely.

Please, preachers, respect your parishioners' time on Sunday mornings. This is another way in which God's Word can be respected. It is possible to allow the Spirit of God to move *and* to leave the service at a reasonable hour. Keeping the Sabbath does not mean routinely keeping parishioners in the eleven o'clock service until dinnertime.[5] I know of one preacher who finds it insulting that anyone would have Sunday activities that include more than church. If he senses anyone stirring, he digs in, preaching as a form of punishment.

Instead of acknowledging that God wants us to live our lives fully and to contribute in a number of venues, or understanding that the church of God is people and not a building, this preacher abuses his position in the pulpit. Some preachers think that church is not meaningful unless they preach for an hour or more. It *is* possible to put meaning into short sermons. These "one hour" preachers seem to suffer from low self-esteem and to forget or not know the lessons we saw in Chapter 2 that encourage preachers to celebrate Christ rather than themselves. Part of how we do that is by respecting the schedules of church members. It also means understanding that God's Word is impeccable: one Word from the Bible is more magnificent, more meaningful, more beautiful than all of our words. So while we all should strive, with our insufficient tongues, to perfect the speaking of God's praise, the preacher should also recognize that there must be a logical limit to the attempt!

don't be eternal

To be immortal, you don't have to be eternal.
—*Gardner C. Taylor*

On the issue of how time is best spent in the pulpit, Rev. Dr. Gardner C. Taylor offered two ideas that many preachers should take to heart. He said, "To be immortal, you don't have to be eternal," and "If you don't strike oil after twenty minutes, stop boring!" In other words, preaching for an hour or more is not required for a sermon to be meaningful to parishioners. As a psychologist with a specialty in learning styles and teaching strategies, I know of a considerable body of research that indicates that learning diminishes in lecture formats beyond twenty minutes. This is something that successful politicians have always known or have been forced to learn. The Gettysburg Address of President Lincoln, considered one of the best speeches in American history, consists of only 268 words and took just two minutes to deliver. Contrast that with the introduction that Arkansas governor Bill Clinton gave presidential candidate Michael Dukakis in 1988. That overly long introduction bored a national television audience for thirty-two minutes. Once Clinton became president, however, he learned to give meaningful messages appropriate to their venues and became renowned for his ability to connect meaningfully with his audiences. A number of preachers whom I have heard could enhance parishioners' attention to and learning from God's Word by the strategic use of sermonic brevity.

preach up a storm

I got a Savior in-a that kingdom,
Ain't-a that good news![6]

We in the pew love to hear good preaching. God's Word inspires and teaches us. It encourages us to live according to God's purpose for our lives. The oratorical skills of the preacher stir up storms in our souls. No tempests in teapots here, no storms stirred up in small places or within diminutive spirits. Good preaching revives our spirits, renews our energies, and enlarges our commitments to God. Preach to us of Christ and his glory. Preach to us so that we are covered in and protected by the blood of the crucified Lamb. Mentor us through preaching: teach us and provide us with the tools to access God's protection. Preach to us, preacher. Leave yourself out of it,[7] and we'll catch up with you at coffee hour!

thoughts from the pulpit

Preacher's Prayer: Dear Lord, it is my prayer to exalt you and you alone in the pulpit. Keep me close to you, that I may truly honor your pulpit and preach your marvelous Word. Amen.

Pastor's Promise: I will seek to be a pastor to the members of my congregation, to preach inspiration and hope through God's Word, to honor the sanctity of the worship service, and to minimize the personal exercise of ego in the pulpit.

Minister's Message: I will organize worship to honor God, while understanding the learning and spiritual needs of my congregants.

thoughts from the pew

Parishioners' Prayer: Our Father and our God, we ask for ears to listen to the deep meaning of your Word and for spirits to incorporate your lessons into our lives. We vow to partner with the pastor in the preaching moment, to connect to the congregation of believers in praise of you, and to honor the worship experience. Amen.

Parishioners' Plea: Dear Pastor, we ask you to be aware of our needs as you seek to honor the Word of God. Feed us God's holy Word in its purest form, support us as we grow in our relationship with Christ, and be with us as members of a Christian community that seeks to live for Christ.

NOTES

1. Glenn Edward Burleigh, "Is There a Word from the Lord?" Copyright © 1998 Glen Burleigh (Burleigh Inspirations Music,

Publisher). Used by special permission. Made in U.S.A. All rights reserved.

2. In other Christian worship services, preaching is not the central component for the service. For example, in Roman Catholic services the Eucharist is central, and in Quaker services the central component of the worship service consists of quiet reflection on the goodness of God.

3. Reinhold Niebuhr, http://www.quotationspage.com (accessed March 14, 2003).

4. Jennie Wilson, "Hold to God's Unchanging Hand," in *African American Heritage Hymnal*, ed. Delores Carpenter and Nolan E. Williams Jr. (Chicago: GIA Publications, 2001), 404. Copyright © by GIA Publications, Inc., Chicago, Illinois. All rights reserved. Used with permission.

5. This trait, I understand, is one that often is regional (Southern), or is attached to the traditions of particular denominations (e.g., African Methodist Episcopal, Baptist, Church of God in Christ, and other Pentecostal groups) or racial and ethnic groups (African Americans).

6. Negro spiritual. "Ain't-a That Good News" in *African American Heritage Hymnal*, ed. Delores Carpenter and Nolan E. Williams Jr. (Chicago: GIA Publications, 2001), 592. Copyright © by GIA Publications, Inc., Chicago, Illinois. All rights reserved. Used with permission.

7. In the same manner that this book makes its points through the use of personal stories, sermons use the technique of teaching through pastoral experience seen through the lens of Scripture. Thus, the statement "leave yourself out of it" refers not to the use of personal stories in preaching, but to the negative, self-serving, soul-stifling misuses of the sermonic moment that have been described in this chapter and will be addressed in other places in the book.

be a shepherd, not a showman

When I survey the wondrous cross,
On which the Prince of Glory died,
My richest gain I count but loss
And pour contempt on all my pride.[1]

TELEVANGELISM HAS CHANGED THE LANDSCAPE OF THE MINISTRY IN several ways. It has developed new strategies for celebrating the good news of Jesus Christ. In some cases it has also shown ministers that pulpit showmanship can be used to enlarge congregations and increase the church's financial resources. On the local level many ministers now are using these showman tactics in their pulpits. I have seen ministers jump out of the pulpit, run through the congregation, stand on chairs, lay themselves prostrate on the altar, throw their coats, crawl over pews—to name a few of the more interesting actions. Any of these actions could be genuine strategies to illustrate God's Word or serve as evidence of the movement of the Holy Spirit in that ministerial moment, but sometimes such things are done just for show. Although preaching is the "performed

41

Word of God," it is not meant to be a performance. The pew can tell the difference.

In the days before television had evangelists on every cable network, the socially important role of the preacher in modern society made it a coveted position for many. The increased visibility has made the role of preacher attractive to some. Congregants in the pews are likely to be wary of calls to the ministry that, when honestly assessed, appear to be fueled primarily by ego, by the need to get in front of a camera, in front of a congregation, up in the pulpit for the purpose of being a showman rather than a shepherd for the Lord. Ego allows God's Word to be interpreted through an inappropriate filter and, in so doing, dishonors the pulpit.

don't be impressed that you preach
Whereof I was made a minister, according to the gift of the grace of God given unto me by the effectual working of his power. (Ephesians 3:7)

The ego of the showman preacher makes it difficult for him or her to see that ministering is a gift, not a talent, and that ministry is a responsibility and privilege, not a boon to the preacher's positive self-perception.

Preachers must preach because God has commanded them to, because God has spoken to them in the depths of their hearts and disciplined their spirits in the boot camp of the Word. Although a certain showmanship assists in helping those in the pew to understand the dramatic ways in which God can move, using showmanship for the purposes of scriptural illustration and being a showman in order to feed the needs of one's ego are not the same thing. Preachers, you are the undershepherds of Christ, and you must use God's Word to teach those in the pews through the sermon. The sermon is a tool for reaching souls and changing lives.

Though preachers often are blessed with multiple gifts that allow them to reach into the hearts of those who need to be brought to Christ, preachers should not allow those gifts for oratory, singing, storytelling, church administration, and relationship building to make their hats too small for their heads or their necks too large for their collars.

don't preach to impress

Unto me, who am less than the least of the saints, is this grace given, that I should preach among the Gentiles the unsearchable riches of Christ. (Ephesians 3:8)

If pastoral head coverings and collars fit, it is because preachers understand that they preach through the grace of God and not because of their own skills. Those in the pew may indeed be impressed by someone whose gifts shine brightly and through whom God speaks clearly, but impressing parishioners should not be the goal of preaching. If the spirit of the message is wrong, God is not glorified.

be dressed to bless

The Lord is blessing me right now.[2]

Respect for oneself in the pulpit and for the pulpit itself also is manifested in how a preacher dresses. In some denominations this is not an issue, as pastors wear the robes of their station in the ministry. However, just as the chief justice of the U.S. Supreme Court found it necessary to adorn his robe with the gold braid worn by a character in Gilbert and Sullivan's

Iolanthe, many a preacher has found a way to make a distinctive appearance on a Sunday morning.

Among Baptists, the autonomous nature of each local church creates an opportunity for preachers to wear what they will—and some of them really do! Don't get me wrong—parishioners appreciate a well-dressed preacher. But preachers, please, skip the flash. We prefer a preacher whose attire is dignified to one whose style resembles that of an entertainer. I once was confronted by a preacher who was dressed like Nathan Detroit, a character from the musical *Guys and Dolls.* I don't want my preacher to be dressed like a gangster or appear to be in costume. Dignity in dress indicates respect for the pulpit and sets a model for appropriate church dress and behavior among parishioners. Preacher, don't display all of your material blessings each Sunday. Too much flash can suggest to parishioners that preaching is entertainment rather than worship.[3]

be humble
Humble yourselves in the sight of the Lord,
and he shall lift you up. (James 4:10)

As viewed from the pew:
  Confidence attracts.
  Humility endears.
  Arrogance distances.
  Performance, rather than preaching, insults.
  Be humble.
  Make it easy for God to work in and through you.

know when to sit down
The preparations of the heart in man, and the answer of the
tongue, is from the LORD. (Proverbs 16:1)

Most preachers love to hear themselves talk, and as a result they sometimes preach too long. We in the pews don't need to be worked into a frenzy. We respond as the Spirit moves us. The second law of thermodynamics states that energy is never lost, but is transferred from place to place—often in forms that we don't recognize. Preacher, if you put out energy through your sermon, it will reach us, even if it is not evident to you. You just need to make sure that when you speak, God is saying something through you. I guarantee that the pew will respond.

be careful what you ask

Jesus answered and said, "Ye know not what ye ask.
Are ye able to drink of the cup that I shall drink of, and to
be baptized with the baptism that I am baptized with?"
(Matthew 20:22)

Being a shepherd means, among other things, being attuned to the personalities, tendencies, and potentials of the sheep for which one is responsible. From the position atop the hill, the astute shepherd can sense the mood of the sheep and, by walking a certain way, direct them along the desired course. This does not suggest pastoral manipulation of those in the pew, but rather refers to the ways that good preachers can sense the mood of the flock and preach to it.

Courtroom lawyers recognize an ironclad rule that one should ask no question to which the answer is not already known. This might be a good rule for preachers to consider as well. There is a new convention in homiletic styling that is increasingly used by preachers. In an attempt to stir emotion or get confirmation and support for the sermonic points they make, preachers ask questions such as "Can I preach?"

45

to get an encouraging congregational response. This can backfire, however. A preacher whose sermon had gone on a bit too long once asked that question, and a man in the balcony responded loudly, "Well, what have you *been* doing?" As an experienced pew-sitter, I can honestly say that congregations usually don't have to be goaded into actively participating in worship. A preacher who feels the need to *make* a congregation respond probably is dealing more with the weak content or the excessive length of the sermon than with a congregation that, despite the preacher's best efforts, is unresponsive to God's Word.

To get congregants actively involved in the worship experience, many preachers are also using a tactic that asks them to repeat a phrase such as "Turn to your neighbor and say...." Though this strategy gets people involved in thinking about sermon content in important ways, it gets quite tiresome when overused, which frequently it is. On several occasions I have counted these requests; the highest number of requested repetitions to date is fifteen in forty minutes. One way to determine request overload is to watch the congregation; if persons you know to be active participants in the service are no longer turning to their neighbors or otherwise honoring preacher requests, regroup and try something new. Or, better yet, don't be a showman. Just preach the Word.

get out of god's way

God is a good God.
He's a great God.
He can do anything but fail.
He has moved so many mountains out of my way.
God is a wonderful God.[4]

Question: How do you get a straw out of a bottle without touching the bottle? *Answer:* You pour water in the bottle and let the straw float out. Sometimes preachers get in the way of God's Word, so intent are they on showing off their preacherly skills. Such behavior is showmanship rather than shepherding. The riddle about the bottle and the straw has an important application to all of our lives, preachers and parishioners alike: the blessings that God has deposited in us are more likely to come out in the form he intends when we get out of the way and let his presence flow into and through us.

use the pulpit well

Do not let your deeds belie your words, lest when you speak in church someone may say to himself, "Why do you not practice what you preach?"[5]

Being a shepherd also means being a model of Christian behavior in and out of the pulpit. Preachers, your behavior outside of the pulpit follows you into it. If you malign parishioners, participate in gossip, or commit other un-Christian actions, such behaviors become a large piece of baggage that you carry into the pulpit. If you're engaging in these behaviors, your parishioners know it. Jesus saves and forgives, but preachers must strive to live godly lives as part of their personal covenant with God, as a model of Christian living for congregants, and as evidence of worthiness to stand before God's people in the position of authority that the pulpit represents.

In a similar manner, preachers who don't enter the pulpit until it's time to preach,[6] who sit in the pulpit and check their e-mail or play games on their computers,[7] who look bored unless they are preaching, or who doze off in their comfortable chairs are sending the message to the pew that they view themselves as more central than Christ to the service of worship and are emotionally disconnected from the sanctity of the moment. Such behaviors show disrespect for the worship experience and indicate that the preacher is interested only in preaching or only in the sound of his or her own voice. This sends poor and confusing theological messages. To be a shepherd means exemplifying integrity. It means engaging the opportunity of preaching.

engage the opportunity of preaching

Casting down imaginations, and every high thing that exalteth itself against the knowledge of God, and bringing into captivity every thought to the obedience of Christ. (2 Corinthians 10:5)

Finally, being a shepherd means engaging the special opportunity that is presented by the very privilege of preaching. The preacher-prophet Howard Thurman[8] often talked about how easy it is to create sermons that are emotive but lacking in content. Preaching is an opportunity to bring God's Word to the people, to use the corporate experience of worship to explore the deeper meaning of the Word, and to connect meaningfully to the needs of God's people gathered for worship. Preaching, through the well-prepared sermon, teaches parishioners the historical, political, and social contexts of the Bible, places the emotional and social challenges of the congregation within a biblical context, uses relevant personal pastoral experiences to create connections with those of parishioners, and presents God's Word in a manner that brings believers to Christ. Preachers, preach sermons rich in content. Engage the learning wishes and spiritual needs of parishioners. Honor God by giving serious consideration to the importance of a well-prepared sermon, to the task of being a shepherd through whom God can speak. This is a high privilege and an awesome responsibility.

thoughts from the pulpit

Preacher's Prayer: My God, as I enter this moment of worship, hide me now but reveal the Christ, so that he might be glorified and his people edified through the mysteries of this preaching moment. Amen.

Pastor's Promise: I will seek to be a pastor to the members of my congregation, to preach from my passion for the Word of God, and to enter the pulpit with humility.

Minister's Message: In my organization of the act of corporate worship I will value preaching that results from sermons rich in content and emotional connectedness to the people of the congregation, working with them to create memorable messages that remain in their hearts and reach God's ear.

thoughts from the pew

Parishioners' Prayer: God, our Father, we seek to learn from your Word. We will listen to and learn from the lessons of sermons, encouraging the preacher of the gospel and engaging with our brothers and sisters in Jesus in the glory that attends the body of Christ on each occasion that we join together in corporate worship. Amen.

Parishioners' Plea: Pastor, we ask for a balanced worship service, one that glorifies God in song, outlines history through Scripture, explains Scripture in the sermon, connects us to one another through congregational activity, and respects our time, understanding that we must be taught to worship in God's house and in the world.

NOTES

1. Isaac Watts, "When I Survey the Wondrous Cross," in *African American Heritage Hymnal,* ed. Delores Carpenter and Nolan E. Williams Jr. (Chicago: GIA Publications, 2001), 243. Copyright © by GIA Publications, Inc., Chicago, Illinois. All rights reserved. Used with permission.

2. Gospel Song, "The Lord Is Blessing Me Right Now," in *African American Heritage Hymnal,* ed. Delores Carpenter and Nolan E. Williams Jr. (Chicago: GIA Publications, 2001), 506. Copyright © by GIA Publications, Inc., Chicago, Illinois. All rights reserved. Used with permission.

3. In a church that my father pastored at one time, pastor and parishioners arrived at Sunday morning services in evening dress. The previous pastor was unmarried, some of the women were seeking husbands, and the services became an odd ritual of "see and be seen."

4. Keith Hunter, "God Is a Good God," in *African American Heritage Hymnal,* ed. Delores Carpenter and Nolan E. Williams Jr. (Chicago: GIA Publications, 2001), 151. Copyright © by GIA Publications, Inc., Chicago, Illinois. All rights reserved. Used with permission.

5. St. Jerome, http://www.quotationspage.com (accessed September 14, 2002).

6. This is a pet peeve of mine. When a preacher enters just before the sermon, it tells me that ego and performance needs have superseded

his or her understanding of the pastoral role. Such preachers appear not to value the Spirit of God as it is shared through the ministry of music, the reading of Scripture, congregational singing, and other acts that exist to build a sense of corporate worship and connected-ness. Sharing the entire service creates a bond between pastor and people that infuses worship with deeper meaning.

7. When talking about preachers using PDAs from the pulpit I need to be clear that many technology-savvy preachers use these devices as techo-Bibles, to record sermons, and to engage in other activities that enhance their capacity to engage the gospel. I am not referring to them or to these specific activities. They may, in fact, walk into the pulpit and place their PDA on the pulpit to use it as notes in much the same way that other preachers use note cards, legal paper, print-outs from their computer files, or sermons sheathed inside manila folders or leather binders. Instead, I am referring to those preachers who are clearly checking e-mail, playing games, or are otherwise staving off boredom in the pulpit, when they should be working to be as engaged as they can be with the activities of the moment.

8. Considered one of the great mystics and theologians of the Twen-tieth Century, Howard Thurman (1900–1981) was a prominent African American pastor and religious leader. Internationally known for his stance of nonviolence and prolific as an author, he pastored The Church for the Fellowship of All Peoples and influ-enced Martin Luther King Jr.'s views on nonviolence.

do the vision thing

Better mind, my sister,
how you walk on de cross,...
Your foot might slip
an' your soul be lost.[1]

GEORGE HERBERT WALKER BUSH, LIKE ALL U.S. PRESIDENTS, WAS CRITI-
cized for his policymaking strategies. In a 1987 press conference President Bush responded to the suggestion that he turn
his attention from short-term campaign objectives and look to
the longer term by saying, "Oh, the vision thing." This statement implied, somewhat derisively, that vision was not a necessary factor in politics. Wrong answer. Meaningful
leadership requires vision.

According to the Encarta dictionary, the word "vision"
derives from a participial form of the Latin word *videre*, "to
see." Among its meanings are the following definitions:

- *Eyesight:* the ability to see
- *Mental picture:* an image or concept in the imagination
- *Something seen in a dream or trance:* an image or series of
  images seen in a dream or trance, often interpreted as having religious, revelatory, or prophetic significance

- *Far-sightedness:* the ability to anticipate possible future events and developments
- *Television picture:* the picture on a television screen
- *Somebody or something beautiful:* a beautiful or pleasing sight.[2]

Although few people are likely to debate the usefulness of vision to the stability of democracy, those who have been called to preach God's Word must be forward-thinking people, men and women of vision whose hearts and minds are additionally open to the vision for service that God may share with them. The preacher's vision must:

- See the needs of the church and congregation clearly (eyesight);
- Imagine local church and congregational growth as steps toward expanding the kingdom of God (mental picture);
- Be responsive to images seen in dreams, responses to prayers, and other signs of revelation or prophecy (something seen in a dream or trance);
- Interpret God's Word, using its guidance to anticipate future events that may impact church life, development, and growth, and, in line with that vision, making plans for necessary developments (far-sightedness);
- Learn social concerns and trends as presented in popular culture and media (television picture);
- View the beauty of God's creation in nature, in God's people, and in oneself (somebody or something beautiful).

be focused

Keep your eyes on the prize, hold on.[3]

Whether we think of it in physiological or metaphorical terms, vision requires that the visionary be focused. Visionaries must keep their eyes directed toward a goal. For the preacher, that goal is determined by prayer and supported by a firm belief in the direction that God leads. On July 28, 2002, Rev. Jawanza Colvin, pastor of the East Friendship Baptist Church of Washington, D.C., preached a sermon about vision. Specifically, he focused on the courage that it takes to follow Jesus. Life, he said, "is not about your function but your focus." This applies greatly to those involved in the vocation of ministry:

- Being a preacher is not about the job but the journey.
- Being a preacher is less about the role than the responsibility.
- Being a preacher is more about the trust than the title.
- Being a preacher is not a function but a focus.
- Being a preacher is about following in the way that Christ leads.
- Being a preacher is about being focused at all times on Christ.

see the big picture

I have a dream.
—Martin Luther King Jr.

Vision and the focus it requires cannot be narrow. True visionaries are highly unlikely to have tunnel vision. For their vision to have any power, they must look above and beyond the mundane. Visionaries must see the big picture and share it with the people of God.

When Martin Luther King Jr. stood in front of the Lincoln Memorial, the dream that he imagined was his vision for a united America. He saw the big picture. Not everyone has the vision of King, but God shares his vision with his people. The preacher's vision must extend to God's plans for the expansion of his kingdom in local congregations and communities and in the larger world. Limiting one's vision can result in limiting the preparation of God's people to receive his blessings.

plan strategically

Howbeit when he, the Spirit of truth, is come, he will guide you into all truth: for he shall not speak of himself; but whatsoever he shall hear, that shall he speak: and he will show you things to come. (John 16:13)

Vision is not necessarily something that shows up full-grown in the preacher's mind. Besides being focused and keeping in mind the big picture, vision requires strategic planning.

What is the relationship between vision and strategy?

John Bryson, the author of *Strategic Planning for Public and Nonprofit Organizations,* states that typically, a vision is "more important as a guide to implementing strategy than it is to formulating it." This is because the development of strategy is driven by what you are trying to accomplish, your organization's purposes. A mission statement answers the questions: Why does our organization exist? What business are we in? What values will guide us? A vision, however, is more encompassing. It answers the question, "What will success look like?" It is the pursuit of this image of success that really motivates people to work together.

A vision statement should be realistic and credible, well articulated and easily understood, appropriate, ambitious, and responsive to change. It should orient the group's energies and serve as a guide to action. It should be consistent with the organization's values. In short, a vision should challenge and inspire the group to achieve its mission.[4]

Within the church, mission and vision, guided by God, look much the same as the factors described by Bryson. The difference between the goals of the church and those of other nonprofit organizations is their specific spiritual aim. The mission of the church responds to the aforementioned questions this way:

- *Why does our organization exist?* To bring souls to Christ and extend his Word into the world.
- *What business are we in?* The business of salvation.
- *What values will guide us?* The life, teaching, and works of Christ.
- *How will we implement those values?* Through a well-designed, monitored, and strategically implemented plan of action to grow the kingdom of God in our church and the community beyond our doors.
- *How will we know that we have met with success?* "He'll understand and say, 'Well done'"[5] (cf. 2 Timothy 4:7-8 and Matthew 25:21).

As a challenge to help the church achieve its mission, those casting the vision must continually ask how we will recognize success in our implementation of God's vision for our churches and our individual lives. At the day of judgment, God will let us know how well or how poorly we have done, but until then, we must simply remain open to the will of God for our lives and accept the blessings that he gives us in response to our faithfulness (cf. Malachi 3:9-11).

embrace god's vision for your vineyard
What God has for me, it is for me.[6]

A broad focus on the goal, an understanding of the big picture, and well-planned strategies for success in the local church and surrounding community are components of God's vision for us that must be enthusiastically embraced by the preacher. The success of God's vision in the local church is seen in the training of congregations through dedicated and well-designed Christian education programs, by the strategic growth of local congregations, in ministries that recognize and serve the needs of God's people, and by powerful preaching that celebrates God, thanks him for his goodness to us, and offers up our hearts as homes for his love.

assert the call
"For many are called, but few are chosen."
(Matthew 22:14)

Having vision also means that if God has truly called you to service, you will learn, through prayer and reflection, what he would have you do.

see what ezekiel saw
Ezekiel saw de wheel, way up in de middle of de air.
Ezekiel saw de wheel, way in de middle of de air.
And de big wheel turns by faith.
And de little wheel turns by the grace of God.
A wheel in a wheel, way in de middle of de air.[7]

The French essayist Montaigne wrote, "Every man carries within himself the history of the world," a record of the triumphs and failures of all of humanity. History builds, of course, by the experience of each person and the sharing of personal, family, and community stories within the collective. In many ways, the book of Ezekiel tells the story of the history of the world that was Israel, captive and troubled. It is Ezekiel's own tale, carrying in it his perceptions of the world in which he lived and his actions within it.

Ezekiel saw visions of many kinds, fantastic and frightening and revelatory. One of his most vivid visions is that of the wheels spinning within each other, on the other side of which was a man, splendidly arrayed and seated on a throne. Ezekiel was certain of this vision; he knew that what he saw was God's glory displayed in the face and form of what would later be interpreted as a Christ-like figure.

Though preachers will hear from God about his plans for their local vineyards, not every preacher will have visions, and among those who do, most will not have the visions of Ezekiel. Nonetheless, preachers do have visionary gifts that can help parishioners see what Ezekiel saw. They can help those of us who sit in the pews build lives, individual and collective, that can add meaningfully to the history of the world that we hold within us and that we create through our daily actions. Preachers, through their gifts, can help us to see, in every display of nature and in every person we meet, God's glory and the radiant face of Christ.

thoughts from the pulpit

Preacher's Prayer: *Open mine eyes that I might see visions of truth Thou has for me; be in my heart, illumine me, Savior divine.*[8] O Lord my God, give me faith to believe, a mind to understand, and the vision to see the blessings that you have in store for the people of God whom I have been called to serve. Grant me a heart that seeks your presence daily, and in my seeing, may I always see you. Amen.

Pastor's Promise: I will be a pastor who sees clearly, stays focused, provides effective modes of biblical training, actively engages the church's mission, understands and ministers to the many needs of my congregation and community, and seeks at every moment the glory of God and the purpose of Jesus for my ministry to others and the salvation of my own soul. With the help of Christ, whom I serve and whose name my every effort should glorify daily, I make this humble promise.

Minister's Message: In my ministry I will plan strategically for church growth and development, working with the leadership of the church to build plans that extend the reach of God's kingdom on earth.

thoughts from the pew

Parishioners' Prayer: We ask, dear Lord, your blessings upon our pastor, and offer a prayer that (he or she) will learn through fervent prayer and strategic study, the vision that you have in store for this congregation. We ask that you guide our pastor's heart and mind, granting (him or her) the wisdom of the elders, the patience of Job, the foresight of the prophets, and the faith of a child. Guide our feet, we pray, while we run this race, for we know that if we heed your call, this race can never be run in vain. Amen.

Parishioners' Plea: Dear Pastor, as you plan, in conjunction with church leadership, for the future of this particular branch of Zion, remember us. Keep these children of God in sight as you use the vision granted you by God to enlarge our portion of the kingdom. We encourage you in the name of Jesus the Christ, under whose cross we live, and whose purpose we serve.

NOTES

1. "Ezekiel Saw de Wheel," in *African American Heritage Hymnal,* ed. Delores Carpenter and Nolan E. Williams Jr. (Chicago: GIA

Publications, 2001), 484. Copyright © by GIA Publications, Inc., Chicago, Illinois. All rights reserved. Used with permission.

2. Keyword "vision," http://encarta.msn.com (accessed September 14, 2002).

3. Author unknown, song of the Civil Rights Movement.

4. http://www.allianceonline.org/FAQ/strategic_planning/what_s_in_vision_statement.faq (accessed November 20, 2003).

5. Lucie E. Campbell, "He'll Understand and Say 'Well Done,'" in *African American Heritage Hymnal*, ed. Delores Carpenter and Nolan E. Williams Jr. (Chicago: GIA Publications, 2001), 413. Copyright © by GIA Publications, Inc., Chicago, Illinois. All rights reserved. Used with permission.

6. Joy Cooper, "It Is for Me," *It's Praying Time* (Miami Mass Choir CD, 1997).

7. "Ezekiel Saw de Wheel," 484.

8. The opening words provided in the "Preacher's Prayer" incorporate text from "Open My Eyes," written and composed by Clara H. Scott in 1895. The full text of "Open My Eyes" follows:

> 1. *Open my eyes, that I may see*
>   *Glimpses of truth Thou hast for me;*
>   *Place in my hands the wonderful key*
>   *That shall unclasp and set me free.*
>   *Silently now I wait for Thee,*
>   *Ready, my God, Thy will to see;*
>   *Open my eyes, illumine me, Spirit divine!*
>
> 2. *Open my ears, that I may hear*
>   *Voices of truth Thou sendest clear;*
>   *And while the wave-notes fall on my ear,*
>   *Everything false will disappear.*
>   *Silently now I wait for Thee,*
>   *Ready, my God, Thy will to see;*
>   *Open my ears, illumine me, Spirit divine!*

3. *Open my mouth and let me bear*
   Gladly the warm truth everywhere;
   Open my heart, and let me prepare
   Love with Thy children thus to share.
   Silently now I wait for Thee,
   Ready, my God, Thy will to see;
   Open my heart, illumine me, Spirit divine!

4. *Open my mind, that I may read*
   More of Thy love in word and deed;
   What shall I fear while yet Thou dost lead?
   Only for light from Thee I plead.
   Silently now I wait for Thee,
   Ready, my God, Thy will to see;
   Open my mind, illumine me, Spirit divine!
   Amen.

CHAPTER 6

expose the pastor in you

Not my mother, not my father,
But it's me, O Lord,
Standin' in the need of prayer.[1]

A FEW YEARS AGO I JOINED A CHURCH IN MY LOCAL COMMUNITY.
Although joining a church is always a momentous occasion,
one that signifies a wish to connect with a community of faith
and to move forward in one's personal spiritual life, this particular event had special importance for me. I had always told
myself that I would not join a church until my father, my first
pastor, died. Church membership was something that I associ-
ated with my father's legacy in the ministry. Even though I had
lived away from home for years, I found it hard to imagine
shifting my church membership while he was alive. But one
Sunday I returned to a church that I had visited several times.
The minister, a young man, was someone known to me
through family connections. Eloquent, well prepared to
preach, and creative in his approach to the messages he deliv-
ered from the pulpit, he was and is a remarkable preacher. The
church, emboldened with the energy of a young congregation,
was near my home and appeared to be a vibrant place that was

spirit-filled and ripe for growth. So one Sunday morning, tears in my eyes for many reasons, I joined.

I was having serious health problems at the time that I joined, though I was managing them well and did not join for any conscious concerns about a need for physical healing. Rather, I had found a church that seemed so strong and so inviting that I was able to reevaluate the promise I had made to withhold church membership because of my love for my father. Something wonderful had happened in this church that made it possible for me to realize that my promise to not officially affiliate with a church was stunting my spiritual growth. Several months after joining, however, my health took a turn for the worst. I was unable to work or to attend church. I called the church office to leave a message for the minister. As a new parishioner and a family friend, I thought it important to let him know that I was ill and to request prayer and a visit. I never heard from him or from anyone in leadership at the church. Several months after my crisis, I got a call from the minister. After we had talked for a while, I asked if he had gotten my earlier message. He stated that he had but that he had not had time to deal with my problems because he was dealing with several of his own. Finding this shocking, I simply finished my conversation with him and never returned to the church. I was certain that in spite of the power of its Sunday morning services, something important was missing.

This entire experience made me feel hurt and angry. More than either of those emotions, however, I was confused. Though I was happy to have felt safe enough within this body of Christ to learn that church membership was vital for my personal spiritual development and to overcome my particular emotional hurdle, I was distraught that in choosing membership in that particular church I had not paid enough attention to something that is essential for a church to be strong, vibrant, and vital: Jesus wants pastors and parishioners to be in relationship with him and with one another. I had not explored something that is the responsibility of all parishioners upon joining with a congregation—I had not adequately investigated the preacher's ability (or inability, in this case) to be in relationship with his parishioners. Good preaching is not enough. Good preachers must also be good pastors.

be pastoral

Feed the flock of God which is among you, taking the oversight thereof, not by constraint, but willingly; not for filthy lucre, but of a ready mind; Neither as being lords over God's heritage, but being ensamples to the flock. (1 Peter 5:2-3)

To be a good pastor requires having an in-depth understanding of this particular ministerial role. The Encarta dictionary defines the word "pastor" as:

- *Minister:* a Christian minister or priest in charge of a congregation.
- *Spiritual adviser:* someone, not always a minister, who provides spiritual guidance to others.
- *Shepherd:* the leader of a flock (congregation).[2]

In the minds of those in the pew, the definition of "pastor" generally focuses on the second and third roles. Parishioners expect their pastors to be their shepherds and spiritual advisers, to be available to them for the important questions of how to structure their lives in the ways that Christ expects, to get them through the tough times and dark days that are sure to come, and to share with them the happy times that are part of our life journeys.

Parishioners have specific expectations of pastors based on their personal needs. People connect to one another through their emotions. Parishioners therefore expect some access to and recognition from their pastors on this emotional level. Church pews are filled with persons who are seeking God for many different reasons. Some are continuing long-term stable relationships with Christ, others are renewing their Christian commitments as a first step in getting their lives back on track, and others are seeking healing for specific physical and psychological ills. Parishioners want their preachers to be shepherds, men and women of God who are led by the Spirit of God and thus can lead, advise, and counsel them. Pastoring is relational; it relies on strong bonds between ministers and their congregations, relationships that are built through shared objectives for living in Christ and the vast array of personal characteristics, situations, and emotional responses that bring people together.

Preachers are possessors of positions of great importance in the world and in my life. Ever curious about how they perceive their roles and conduct their work, I listen as they describe their lives. Some of them, I have learned, are confused about what it means to be a pastor of their flock. For example, one minister related to me his absolute admiration for several giants in the ministry, all of whom I knew well. He stated his wish to be like them because they were so well loved by their congregations. This love I viewed as respect earned by these men as a result of years of faithful service to their congregations. The minister hypothesized that this was because they were theological scholars, eloquent wordsmiths, superb musicians, and preachers par excellence. I could not disagree with his assessment of their phenomenal skills in these areas—God's hand was on them in undeniably evident ways. But I had another idea about why they were so well loved by their congregations, one that I knew to be true. Having spent considerable amounts of time in all of their churches, it was clear to me that the love that surrounded them included an acknowledgment of their particular ministerial gifts; but more than that, they were loved because they were superb pastors.

I recalled that one of the pastors took special notice one morning of a senior saint who had returned to the church after a long illness. He admired her hat, smilingly noted that he had lost a few pounds during the time that she had been unable to ply him with her pound cake, and recalled a solo that she had movingly sung as a young woman in the church. This human acknowledgment and connection did not involve his scholarship, musicianship, or preaching; it was excellent pastoring. This minister recognized the history of this woman and her importance to the church. He described the components of a long-time personal relationship with her. He recognized her in public, noticing her in a large crowd and calling her name aloud. Whereas many others saw only an older woman, he saw someone who had made a difference in his life and the life of the church. In a moment of powerful teaching, the pastor educated the congregation; he taught them that his perch was not so high that he did not see his flock and know about their lives. The lovely older lady beamed a glorious smile. In that moment the church learned the important lesson that ministers are servants of God who are called on to tend to the diverse needs of God's people.

Here is another example of pastoral excellence: My sister was a member of a moderately sized church in the community where she lived. I once attended services with her when I was visiting. The music was average but spirited, as was the preaching. Why, I asked, did she attend? As I was asking, the preacher approached me and introduced himself to me. He asked if I had filled out a visitor's card. I indicated that I had. The following week, he called me at my home. Having heard that I had been ill, he offered a prayer for my health. Preaching was not this minister's most special gift; pastoring was. His church was filled every Sunday because his messages, though not distinctive in their presentation, were the offerings of a man who demonstrated his love of God by loving God's people.

earn the trust of the pew
Woe be unto the pastors that destroy and scatter the sheep of my pasture! saith the LORD. (Jeremiah 23:1)

The role of pastor is one that a preacher must want and must actively develop. However, it is also a role that must be earned through actions. Just asking those in the pew to call you pastor is insufficient. Instead, we will know it by what you do. If the church has active ministries that meet the needs of the congregation, we will see the pastor in you. If your sermons preach of kindred love, sharing stories that expose your heart and demonstrate the pastor in you, we will know that you are someone who can be trusted with our deepest secrets. If you share your vulnerabilities as a human being called by God to pastor his people, we will trust you and gladly call you pastor.

My pastor, Rev. Dr. H. Beecher Hicks Jr., a mentor to many in the ministry, shares these words about the importance of trust to creating a shepherd-flock relationship:

> Credibility and trust are not developed overnight. They are the result of months and years of interaction. Every Watchperson on the wall is not trusted on his or her first night on the wall. They may call you "Pastor" but until you have been through trial and tribulation and

have been weighed and found faithful, you are just another preacher.[3]

Dr. Hicks also thinks that those in the pew are more likely to trust a preacher who fosters in the church an atmosphere of trust:

> An atmosphere that encourages the congregation to express honestly their feelings and engage in honest dialogue must exist so that mutual respect will abound throughout the church.... The church must be encouraged to create an environment of wholesome prayer in which acceptance, forgiveness and love can grow. It is only in such an environment that the vision that God intends for the church can be nurtured for the benefit of the entire community.[4]

In many ways, being a pastor is harder than being a preacher. "There are many who want the pleasure of preaching without the pain of pastoring."[5] Pastoring will cause preachers to cry, to mourn, and to grieve, but it will also provide moments for great joy. Pastors, we in the pews love you and ask you, plead with you, to pastor us in all the moments of our lives and to grow with us as one body in Christ.

pastor through preaching
I therefore, the prisoner of the Lord, beseech you that ye walk worthy of the vocation wherewith ye are called. (Ephesians 4:1)

Though being a pastor may be more challenging than the also challenging role of being the preacher, dedication to the pastoral role can also be demonstrated through the preached word. Parishioners have expectations for sermons that are meaningful and moving, but pastors are also responsible for reading the spiritual level of their congregations in the context of worship and in all of the other activities in the church. This involves providing sermons that:

- *Meet congregational learning needs.* The members of congregations are in different places on their journeys toward Christ. Good pastors understand who is in the pews (e.g., new members, persons in recovery from difficult life circumstances, experienced Christians, persons with limited education, professionals) and use the preaching moment to reach them in meaningful ways.

- *Respect the lives and experiences of parishioners.* Ministers must be sensitive to social and emotional factors that impact their parishioners. When preachers make statements that denigrate God's people (blame victims of abuse for their situations, ridicule specific groups, display ignorance of important issues despite available information), parishioners become hurt and confused. The words used in a sermon should not add to the pain parishioners already feel.

- *Enhance the relationship between pastor and people by sharing personal moments.* Preachers use stories to make points important to the theme of their sermons. When preachers share stories from their own lives, parishioners learn that preachers are human and are able to use pastoral experience to inform their own problem solving.

say my name, say my name
Good name in man and woman, dear my lord,
 Is the immediate jewel of their souls.
Who steals my purse steals trash; 'tis something, nothing;
'Twas mine, 'tis his, and has been slave to thousands;
But he that filches from me my good name
Robs me of that which not enriches him,
And makes me poor indeed.[6]

Exposing the pastor in you might mean exposing your very depths, your ministerial genes, and connecting to those in the pew in the deepest possible ways. I am convinced that churches have DNA, complex organizational histories and structures that influence their relationship with pastors and their readiness to act on church initiatives. Not all preachers understand the importance of relationship building in the interactions between pastor and people. Preachers, just as you become pastors when you recognize your parishioners, tend to their spiritual needs, and make emotional connections by sharing personal stories, it is essential that you:

- *Understand the history of your church.* Each church has established internal programmatic and organizational traditions as well as a history within its local community. Understanding these traditions facilitates the building of relationships inside and outside the church.
- *Be aware of the social context of the church.* Who employs your members? What resources educate them? What is the history of your local community? Given this history, what are they likely to need? Understanding social context and how its changes have been felt within the local congregation are factors that inform strategic planning efforts of your church. It also facilitates the mission and vision, assists in the implementation of ministries, and, in general, allows ministers to understand what factors influence the lives of the members who comprise the church in ways that should create meaningful connections to them. For example, if you understand that your membership has come primarily from a particular region of the United States and engages in the traditions of that part of the country, that information should be essential to how you work with your flock. If your congregation is youthful and is primarily new to

Christ, this lets you know that you must organize your new members' ministry in a manner that will train them to understand the faith in ways that would not be required if the membership were made of more-established Christians.

- *Know your parishioners by name.* Though we have told Jesus that it's all right to change our names, we expect you to know them. Recognize us as church members and worthy children of our heavenly Father. Among church members interviewed for this book, there were several complaints about preachers who did not think it important to learn the names of their church members. Or, if these preachers happened to simply have bad memories, parishioners wanted the acknowledgement of a smiling "dear" or other endearment that let them know that they had been *seen.* One woman, so excited to introduce her young son to the preacher, reported that she was simply waved away when she approached him after church. Her two-year-old son had been practicing a greeting for the preacher and did not get an opportunity to shake the preacher's hand. This young mother, a community leader and established and generous tither, found this lack of personal recognition a larger sign of impersonal issues within the church and, wanting a more relational pastor, took her membership elsewhere.

- *Acknowledge your place on the roll.* Unless you have planted a church, it is important to know the history of the pastorate in the place you have been called to serve. What was the tenure of each pastor, and what did he or she accomplish during that time? How can you build on their successes? What is your special place in the church's current and overall history? At the Second Calvary Baptist Church in Virginia Beach, Virginia, one minister had left the church under a cloud. Rev. Gilbert G. Campbell, the current minister, made certain that this man's portrait was displayed along with those of other previous pastors. This illustrated to members that although portions of this former pastor's tenure were problematic, he was a part of the church's history and therefore deserved acknowledgment. The pulpit of Metropolitan Baptist Church in Washington, D.C., lists the names of all of its pastors on the pulpit. The name of the current pastor is in the center, reflecting an awareness of those who preceded him and an understanding that he will be followed by others.

know your strengths
"And ye shall know the truth,
and the truth shall make you free." (John 8:32)

Exposing the pastor in you suggests that it is essential that each preacher work as hard as possible to demonstrate his or her pastoral side. That said, we in the pew understand that not everyone can be the model pastor that so many parishioners seek. To use sports as an analogy, there are some all-star players who make terrible coaches because they focus narrowly on a goal or skill that serves only some of the players well. Other coaches, who are not the best players, have the overarching vision to see how different parts of the team work together effectively and efficiently. The same is true for ministers. Some who have received God's call are excellent administrators who serve their churches well by designing and actively supporting ministries that meet congregational and community needs. Some are superb pastors, serving effectively as counselors and personally tending to the emotional and spiritual needs of their parishioners. Some are dynamic preachers who bring excitement to the retelling of the Christian stories. Some especially gifted men and women of God have all of these skills, but most ministers do not, and they are much more likely to do one ministerial role excellently. No matter what the ministerial talent, preachers must identify and support their internal pastors to intentionally call upon the impulse to connect meaningfully to parishioners in their particular places on individual and corporate spiritual journeys. Finally, ministers for whom preaching is a primary gift should surround themselves with those gifted at administration and pastoring in order to ensure the smooth functioning of the church of God and to strengthen the capacity of their local church to meet congregational needs.

Pastor Is
—Roy Lessin
A pastor is an unusual person, indeed!
He gets his assignments from a voice no one else can hear.
He works for a bonus check
    that is only legal and tendered in heaven.
He starts his day in the prayer closet
    instead of the wardrobe closet.
He climbs the ladder of success by taking the lowly place.
He receives nourishment by feeding sheep.
His greatest gains come by what he gives away.
He is more attracted to what people look like inwardly
    than outwardly.
He lives for God's approval
    rather than following the opinions of others.
He speaks from the depths of his heart
    rather than from the top of his head.
His richest treasures come from the
    investments he makes in the lives of others.[7]

expose the pastor in you

Take heed therefore unto yourselves, and to all the flock, over the which the Holy Ghost hath made you overseers, to feed the church of God, which he hath purchased with his own blood. (Acts 20:28)

Those in the pew recognize a pastor when they see and experience one. Having grown up with a father who was a wonderful pastor, I have been able to discern what parishioners look for in this area of ministerial service. One of the reasons that parishioners love my father is that he allows himself to be vulnerable in the pulpit. He cries at the loss of members of his flock. He is angered by injustices in the world. He smiles and laughs heartily at the funny faces made by the children whom he blesses. When he prayed at my ordination as a deacon, his pride in me and his awareness of the importance of my new role to the life of the church caused his voice to crack and tears to well up in his eyes. In my church, a place where he was a visitor, the words of his prayer and his emotional response moved people greatly. People whom I had never met before ask about him regularly now and mention often that his prayer was one of the most moving that they had ever heard.

My grandmother's minister is also a superb pastor. My grandmother, a devoted churchgoer and respected choir member for over fifty years, died a tragic accidental death. Her pastor, clearly distressed at her loss, preached the eulogy. What affirmed for me his pastoral gift occurred as the service was ending. The congregation stood as the pallbearers prepared to remove my grandmother's casket from the church. Just as the pallbearers began their exit, the minister stopped them with a quiet movement of his hand. He stood in front of my grandmother's coffin and, with his voice quavering, sang to her a beautiful folk song with a history several hundred years old. In doing so, he demonstrated his love for her and created for our family a memory that was healing at such a difficult and unexpected time. He allowed himself to be human and vulnerable. He was pastor to all of us. And though I had felt it all along, that one moment let me know that in her many years of membership in this church, my grandmother's soul had been well tended.

Preachers, you will preach better, you will have sermons more filled with pathos, joy, and the vast array of emotions that make us human, if you expose the pastor in you.

thoughts from the pulpit

Preacher's Prayer: *I am thine, Oh Lord. I have heard Thy voice.*[8] I seek your will for my work among your people. Keep me ever mindful of their needs and the desires of their hearts so that I, like a good shepherd, may lead them to the solace of your Spirit and the salvation of your throne. Amen.

Pastor's Promise: I will seek to be a pastor to the members of my congregation, one who demonstrates my love for God by loving and serving God's people. I understand that in my relationship with members of the congregation, I must show my humanity and not be afraid to demonstrate my vulnerability. In order to provide essential support to God's people and to ensure the smooth functioning of my local congregation, I will surround myself with staff skilled at all aspects of ministering.

Minister's Message: Good pastors preach with purpose, counsel with consideration, listen with love, and serve with selflessness. I seek God's strength in my quest to be a pastor to my parishioners.

thoughts from the pew

Parishioners' Prayer: Our Father, which art in heaven, we ask your special blessings on our pastor and all pastors. We ask that you touch the humanity in their hearts, guide the wisdom with which they make decisions, and grant them the patience to pastor a people with many needs. We need our pastor, Lord, for it is (his or her) work to strengthen us so that your work will be done, your commandments obeyed, and your Word understood. The body of Christ is a family, and we, your children, seek the support that will help our pastor pray this prayer: "Keep me strong in your faith, dedicated to your Word, and faithful to the people whom I have been called to serve. Amen."

Parishioners' Plea: Pastor, we know that you are human, and we love you for it. Show us who you are, and let us love you as you are.

NOTES

1. Negro spiritual, "Standin' in the Need of Prayer."
2. Keyword "pastor," http://encarta.msn.com (accessed July 24, 2002).
3. H. Beecher Hicks Jr., *On Jordan's Stormy Banks* (Grand Rapids: Zondervan, Spring 2004), 266 (in draft).
4. Ibid., 273.
5. Samuel Berry McKinney.
6. William Shakespeare, *Othello,* act 3, scene 3.
7. Roy Lessin, "Pastor Is," accessed at www.dayspring.com.
8. Fanny J. Crosby, "I Am Thine," in *African American Heritage Hymnal,* ed. Delores Carpenter and Nolan E. Williams Jr. (Chicago: GIA Publications, 2001), 387. Copyright © by GIA Publications, Inc., Chicago, Illinois. All rights reserved. Used with permission.

CHAPTER 7

connect
the head and the heart

When peace, like a river, attendeth my way,
When sorrows, like sea billows, roll;
Whatever my lot, Thou hast taught me to say,
It is well, it is well with my soul.[1]

HERE IS A STORY ABOUT FAITH, ONE THAT I HAVE LIVED AND THAT I have written about in fictional form. In my unpublished novel, the character Emma Gautier is asked to recall the most important lesson of her childhood. It is this: "Love God with open hands." The first remembered Bible story of Emma's childhood is the biblical saga of Abraham and Isaac. When commanded by God to sacrifice the promised son of his old age, Abraham never asked God why. His faith allowed him to offer his child to God with open hands and a willing heart. As Abraham prepared to slay his son, God, rewarding Abraham's faith, courage, and obedience, spared the boy. As preparation for how to live a balanced life, one that combined love of God with love of family and friends, Emma's father made this statement to her throughout her childhood: "Don't hold on too tightly to things you love. Offer them to God with open hands." This offering of what is precious to us is of value to God. The openness of our hearts allows God in and helps us experience the beauty of the world he created for us.

I occasionally imagine using the lesson taught by Emma's father as a congregational activity. In this activity, the preacher asks the members of the congregation to consider the things that they have held on to too tightly for reasons of fear, vanity, overpowering love, pride, or something too complicated to immediately grasp. Once these things are identified, the congregants, at their own pace, take them to the altar and symbolically leave them there. This worship activity fantasy is meaningful to me because in my own quiet way, I try to do it each time I enter the sanctuary. I believe the song that says, *"Take your burdens to the Lord and leave them there."* Holding on to my spiritual springtime, I also want to do more than give God what I no longer need, want, or can handle. With open hands and a willing heart, I want to offer up to God my very best, recognizing that it is already his and that my acknowledgment of its true ownership frees me.

The goal of spiritual release is a worthy one, one toward which preachers can encourage their congregations. Preaching (and excellent pastoring) helps those of us in the pew connect our heads and hearts. It helps us understand that Christ sees and accepts us as whole beings who are in need of his love. Sermons that teach, behavior that sets an example, and support that touches church members and ministries can help parishioners avoid the pain of the soul's wintry death, remind them that Jesus will shoulder their burdens, and give them the strength to take their burdens to the Lord and leave them there.

serve balanced meals

*"Meal" (noun): a substantial amount of food, often
more than one course, that is provided and eaten
at one time; from a prehistoric Germanic word, "mal,"
meaning "time, occasion."*[2]

Preachers help those in the pew to connect the head and the
heart by understanding their many spiritual and earth-
bound needs and helping them learn to balance them.
Parishioners come to church to be fed. They arrive at
church with hungers and needs. Parishioners ask preachers
to fill their plates with nutritious spiritual meals of substantial amounts of the Word, served in song, prayer, and
sermons that are manna from God's heaven and that nour-
ish their souls.

count your p's

*The Minstrel Boy to the war is gone,
In the ranks of death you'll find him;
His father's sword he hath girded on,
And his wild harp slung behind him;
"Land of Song!" cried the warrior bard,
"Tho' all the world betrays thee,
One sword, at least, thy right shall guard,
One faithful harp shall praise thee!"*[3]

Connecting the head and the heart also involves, for the pulpit and, through the pulpit's help, the pew, determining how
each us of best serves God. It requires a preacher who understands and teaches us that God does not always call us to a
place of service, but sometimes to engage, wherever we are,
in a process, a purpose, a prayer, and a plan in God's name.

The preaching place is the church, the process is the relationship (between the preacher and God, and the preacher and the parishioners), the purpose is salvation, the prayer is for sanctification and saving grace, and the plan is the sermon. Count your *P*'s, and throw in a *Q* for "quality." As in the case of the minstrel boy, glory is in the process of, purpose for, prayer in support of, and plans related to the faithfulness of our praise.

managing anger
"If you fight from the pulpit,
you will create warriors in the pews."[4]

Leroy Howe has written a book entitled *Angry People in the Pews: Managing Anger in the Church.* Written for pastors, *Angry People in the Pews* is about pastoral care and implies, starting with its title, that people in the pews have strong emotions to which effective pastors must pay attention. As has been dealt with in other chapters of this book, preachers should not feed pew fires with their own personal issues. As my grandfather taught my father, "If you fight from the pulpit, you will create warriors in the pews." Howe's book focuses on ways that pastors can use theology and sermonic strategies to help their parishioners deal with the emotions and issues that they bring into the church.

The feelings of the people in the pew are a component of why we are in God's house. Those issues are many. Parishioners bring the wounds of broken relationships, childhood sexual abuse, domestic violence, HIV/AIDS, homelessness, mental illness, aimlessness, joblessness, and a variety of other hurts. We seek Gilead's balm, and we ask for a pastoral hand in healing our hearts, minds, spirits, and souls.[5]

speak to our hearts

Whatever my lot, Thou hast taught me to say,
It is well, it is well with my soul.[6]

Yet another uniting of our minds and spirits is accomplished when preachers speak to our hearts. A component of each sermon is the exegesis of Scripture, but for many of us in the pew the sermon comes alive only when we can understand it in the context of real life and, more personally, our own lives.

The story of the song "It Is Well with My Soul" is a familiar one that teaches the importance of keeping head and heart connected as a path to Christ's love. Horatio G. Spafford, a successful Chicago attorney, planned a European vacation for his family in the fall of 1873. Detained by business, he sent his wife, Anna, and their four daughters ahead on the SS *Ville du Havre*. With plans to join them soon, he wished them a safe journey. It was not to be. Struck by an English ship in the middle of the Atlantic, the *Ville du Havre* sank, drowning all four Spafford girls. Anna Spafford miraculously survived, kept afloat by a piece of debris. Devastated by the news, Horatio Spafford boarded a ship to travel to his wife, now in Wales. In his hours on board, in the midst of his pain, he felt the presence of God and wrote the song that has comforted countless others for well over a century.

Parishioners know that God will meet us in our hours of need, but we also need the guidance of those whom God has called and trained to minister to us. Those of us in the pew need preachers who will encourage us in our darkest hours, who will sit with us in our pain, who will direct us through prayer to God's throne, who will jump for joy with us, and who are genuinely concerned about our welfare. We need preachers who pastor through preaching, and who, recognizing the needs and directions of individual and corporate spiritual growth, use the rich and unique qualities of God's wonderful Word to speak through our minds to the needs of our hearts.

thoughts from the pulpit

Preacher's Prayer: God of our ancestors, in every moment, remind me of the perfection of your creation—the world you have made and the people who dwell therein. Help me find words that speed healing, prayers that bring comfort, and a heart capable of divining your word in the midst of pain, progress, potential, and powerlessness. When I am not up to the task, support me. Help me to keep my head and my heart connected, and to keep them both trained on you. In gratitude, I will praise your name throughout ceaseless ages; world without end. Amen.

Pastor's Promise: As I work in the ministry, I will be mindful of the special task of pastors to listen to and learn from parishioners, to support the emotional needs of congregants, and to seek God's guidance for my pastoral service through prayer.

Minister's Message: As I serve as chief administrator of the church, I will seek to create ministries that serve the needs of my congregation for healing and health, for wellness and wholeness, for purpose in service and prosperity in spirit.

thoughts from the pew

Parishioners' Prayer: Lord God, support our pastor, we pray, in the task of guiding us toward the throne of grace. Often what we know and what we do are different. Help us in our task of keeping our head and our heart connected, and in making certain that our head and our heart lean toward your Word, send prayers to your throne, and do work in the world on your behalf. We will sometimes fail, but help us always to try mightily. Amen.

Parishioners' Plea: Pastor, serve as intercessor for us. Help us to articulate what we may have trouble saying; remind us that God loves us flaws and all. Help us to remain honest in our relationship with our Savior, who, already knowing our weaknesses, has forgiven our faults and seen to our needs.

NOTES

1. Horatio G. Spafford, "It Is Well with My Soul," in *African American Heritage Hymnal,* ed. Delores Carpenter and Nolan E. Williams Jr. (Chicago: GIA Publications, 2001), 377. Copyright © by GIA Publications, Inc., Chicago, Illinois. All rights reserved. Used with permission.
2. Keyword "meal," http://encarta.msn.com (accessed July 27, 2002).
3. Thomas Moore, "The Minstrel Boy." This rebel song of the United Irishmen was written by Moore following the death of two of his close friends in a war that many believed to be wrong. The young minstrel boy sang of freedom from oppression; the writer expressed satisfaction that the beauty of his music would not be heard in a society that enslaved his people.
4. Rev. Dr. Wade Hampton McKinney Jr., deceased, former pastor, Antioch Baptist Church, Cleveland, Ohio.
5. Leroy Howe, *Angry People in the Pews: Managing Anger in the Church* (Valley Forge, Pa.: Judson Press, 2001).
6. Spafford, "It Is Well with My Soul," 377.

CHAPTER 8

stand on the shoulders of the saints

Wherever I am, there's always Pooh,
There's always Pooh and me.
Whatever I do, he wants to do,
"Where are you going to-day?" says Pooh:
"Well, that's very odd 'cos I was too.
"Let's go together," says Pooh, says he.
"Let's go together," says Pooh.[1]

WHY DO I LOVE WINNIE-THE-POOH STORIES? POOH IS THE ULTIMATE friend, always looking for ways to share special moments with those he loves and absolutely committed to learning from them. Pooh recognizes his limitations. He knows that what he lacks, his friends have; and that what they need, he may well be able to supply. At any rate, together, they will make it through all obstacles.

Pooh's attitude is a wonderful model for living. Whenever I watch Pooh movies, I am reminded that there is always someone to sing my songs, hold my hand, laugh at my silliness, race balloons up trees with me, and dig me out of holes that I fall into looking for the promise of honey.

Life's Pooh-ness is also a way to consider how preachers can learn from each other, building collectively on the skills, perceptions, ideas, and techniques of those especially gifted or those particularly wise from time spent in the Master's vineyard. I once walked into New York City's Abyssinian Baptist Church. Delayed by my Brooklyn train, I arrived late, walking in during the sermon. Rev. Calvin Butts was preaching. A brilliant preacher, he was winding his way into a story. Noticing me, he stopped. "I should mention," he told the congregation, "that the story I'm telling you is not original to me. I heard it first from the father of that young woman right there, the one walking in *late!*" The humor notwithstanding, Rev. Butts did something important. He acknowledged the significance of someone senior to him in the ministry; he thanked my father for his contributions and for what he had learned from him. Doing this publicly taught the pew a valuable lesson: even giants have mentors. Even masters can learn.

preacher, know thyself
This above all: to thine own self be true.[2]

As Winnie-the-Pooh knows only too well, it is important to know exactly who you are in this world. Knowing who you are helps you maintain your authentic self, to understand who you are in relationship to others. Self-knowledge also has another important purpose: it teaches you what you need to learn from others.

Learning from others is important, and it is best preceded by honest self-assessment, strengths and weaknesses alike. An example of the importance of self-knowledge to excellent preaching and pastoring is a preacher whom I heard discuss his ten-year odyssey to find the preaching style that best fit his call, training, obligations, and personality. He had spent a lot of time copying the emotive style of other preachers, and in doing so, he used his voice in ways damaging to his vocal cords, and he repeated, nearly verbatim, sermons that had received wonderful responses. His church grew bit by bit, but he could tell that he was not really connecting with the congregation. One day, throat sore from whooping in an overly low register and too tired to be someone else, he tried something original: he did his own thing. His own thing was to preach in a quiet, intense style, punctuated by an expert knowledge of Greek that allowed him to teach his parishioners important lessons from the biblical text's original language. As a biblical scholar, he also was able to pull stories from the history of God's people, demonstrating in his sermons their continued relevance. That he did not need to have a highly emotive style became clear as people joined his congregation in droves. He connected to them by being prepared to preach and by being genuine in presenting himself to the congregation. This preacher finally understood that learning from others does not mean *becoming* them. Rather, it means incorporating their lessons into one's own identity, into the voice that one has been given by God. It means being real.

search for mentors
Your shallowest help will hold me up afloat.[3]

One way to know ourselves, to identify our authentic selves, is to see ourselves through the eyes of others. All of us, in the pulpit and in the pew, must seek to learn from our seniors and from those whose lives are rich with experience. As we saw in the case the preacher who worked hard to find his appropriate preaching voice, we should emulate, not imitate.

In Homer's *Odyssey*, Odysseus leaves his household under the care of Mentor,[4] who is both teacher and protector of Odysseus's son Telemachus. Mentors provide preachers with teaching: information about Scripture, critiques of sermons, and advice about how best to manage the administrative functions of the church. They also provide protection: vastly experienced preachers themselves, they guide less-experienced preachers around the potholes and alert them to problems. Also, given their broader experience, mentors serve as an additional set of evaluative eyes for understanding issues experienced by those in their care.

The Rev. Dr. Gardner C. Taylor is a senior saint and preacher-teacher-pastor *par excellence*. In his capacity as mentor, he has provided many preachers with invaluable information, tools of the trade, and advice. One of his most important lessons is that the pulpit, no matter whether it is assigned or the result of election to office, must be earned. Dr. Taylor says that the new minister is not truly the pastor when first elected or installed, but *becomes* pastor only as time passes, as respect and love grow in the hearts of his or her people.[5]

Dr. Taylor is a unique and irreplaceable pastoral asset, and there are many other qualified persons who can serve as mentors, not just to new pastors, but also to any who feel that they still have something to learn. For preachers, ministerial mentors are readily available in local communities and seminaries, through relationships built in professional and denominational affiliations, and by recommendations from those who know the learning needs of a particular preacher. People love to share their experiences. Sorting out their life's lessons is as useful to them as it is to those who learn from them. Seeking a mentor—standing on the shoulders of the saints—is an important mechanism for preparing for the pulpit, for effective pastoring, and for relating well to those who comprise the congregation.

be blessed
Blest be the tie that binds Our hearts in Christian love.[6]

Effective mentoring is, in many ways, a blessing from God, one that has an impact on the preacher and, as a result, on those who sit in the pew. One young preacher made certain to note the importance of his mentoring experiences in one of his sermons. Preaching about the changes over time in the ways we praise God, Rev. Emil Thomas of Zion Baptist Church in Washington, D.C., made the point that young people often expect obedience to their wishes and directives but are not willing to be obedient to members of the generation that preceded them. Preachers have much to learn from those senior to them in the ministry. As Rev. Thomas puts it, "Someone was saved before you, preached before you, prayed before you, and was doing God's work before you received your call to ministry."

Older ministers have knowledge that they are happy to share with less-experienced preachers. Their memories contain the jewels of the journey of ministry. Sit at their feet and be blessed.

be a mentor
"Mentor": the task of acting as a mentor to somebody, especially a junior colleague.[7]

Just as everyone has something to learn, everyone has something to teach. As our seniors can teach us and in doing so deliver to us God's unexpected and undeserved blessings, preachers of all levels of experience can serve as mentors—teachers and protectors—to those with less experience. All through their ministry, ministers should be mentored by those with greater experience, and should likewise make themselves available as mentors to those with less experience. This mentoring synergy can create a confidence that contributes to excellent preaching, church administration, and pastoring.

A. A. Milne wrote the Winnie-the-Pooh series to teach important life lessons to his son, Christopher Robin. One of the most important lessons taught through his many books is that a person gets friends by being a friend, and that once friendships are formed, they remain with us in our hearts and minds. One might also become a mentor by being a mentor, and by creating an environment of learning through a process of "give and take" that remains for all time with both the mentor and the one being guided.

"Let's go together," says Pooh, says he. "Let's go together," says Pooh.[8]

thoughts from the pulpit

Preacher's Prayer: Dear Jesus, help me to seek and find those whose age and experience in their work on your behalf inform their wisdom and vision. May I be open to learning from them, transforming their lessons through prayer into content meaningful to my life and ministry. With humility, may I grow in wisdom so that my learning, teaching, preaching, and pastoring will be a blessing to the next generation of ministers for Christ. Amen.

Pastor's Promise: I will seek to be a pastor to the members of my congregation who learns from those who have toiled for generations in God's vineyard.

Minister's Message: As a minister, it is important that I model the value of respect for my elders and demonstrate a humble spirit. No matter how great or small our gifts, we all have something important to learn from the experience and wisdom of others.

thoughts from the pew

Parishioners' Prayer: Gracious God, in these times of rampant selfishness and perspectives limited to the importance of "I," bring into our pulpit your seasoned servants. Help us to learn much from their experiences. Train us for service through their lives of devotion. Through their knowledge of the Word gained from years of study, bring to us and to our pastor new perspectives that will enrich our walk with you. Amen.

Parishioners' Plea: Dear Pastor, we grow in our spiritual walks by hearing a variety of voices and views. Our wish to learn from others does not diminish our capacity or desire to learn from you. Instead, it demonstrates our trust in you and our knowledge that you want for us rich and varied religious experiences. Share other preachers with us so that we can broaden our spiritual horizons and thus be better prepared to understand God's Word.

NOTES

1. A. A. Milne, "Us Two," in *The Christopher Robin Story Book* (New York: E. P. Dutton, 1966), 132.
2. William Shakespeare, *Hamlet,* act 1, scene 3.
3. William Shakespeare, *Sonnets,* 80.
4. Keyword "mentor" is defined in noun form as "teacher and protector," http://encarta.msn.com (accessed March 19, 2003).

5. The Rev. Dr. Gardner C. Taylor states it this way: "Some churches have to be built, but most had to be won by the pastor." In another example, the late Miles Mark Fisher (former pastor, White Rock Baptist Church, Durham, North Carolina) once said to a fledgling pastor, "Young man, don't use your influence until you get it."

6. John Fawcett, "Blest Be the Tie That Binds," in *African American Heritage Hymnal,* ed. Delores Carpenter and Nolan E. Williams Jr. (Chicago: GIA Publications, 2001), 341. Copyright © by GIA Publications, Inc., Chicago, Illinois. All rights reserved. Used with permission.

7. Keyword "mentor" also defined in verb form as "the task of acting as a mentor to somebody, especially a junior colleague," http://encarta.msn.com (accessed March 19, 2003).

8. Milne, "Us Two," 132.

CHAPTER 9

view yourself
from the pew

O wad some Pow'r the giftie gie us
To see oursels as others see us.[1]

KNOWN AS THE "POET OF ALL HUMANITY" FOR HIS VIEWS ON FREE-
dom during a period of colonization and his early support of
the rights of women and other oppressed groups, Robert
Burns (1759–1796), the national poet of Scotland, wrote a
poem, some lines of which are quoted above, about our
human incapacity to consistently and honestly see how we
appear to others. In "To a Louse: On Seeing One on a Lady's
Bonnet in Church," Burns writes about a woman in church
who wore a fancy bonnet, piled high with ribbons and flow-
ers—the absolute height of fashion for a woman of some
wealth. This woman, who was napping during worship, used
fashion to demonstrate her high social standing. Though she
did not know it, her social pretensions were being mightily
undermined by the fact that a louse was merrily crawling
through her hat's decorations. Dressed to the nines and feeling
superior to those around her, she was unaware that she was

home to a parasitic insect, which in poetic form, was also reflective of her spirit.

Then there was the emperor whose only desire was to be well dressed. Though his office required attention to the needs of the people who inhabited his realm, he was focused on impressing his subjects by wearing a different brightly colored coat each hour of the day. The capital city was a center for trade, which, not surprisingly, attracted a number of swindlers. Aware that big-city people liked to dress nicely and of the particular couture requirements of this emperor, some "weavers" had begun trafficking in very special fabrics. Their fabrics, they said, were tremendously beautiful, but were invisible to the unpardonably stupid or to those not suited for their office. The emperor wanted his suits to be made of such fabrics so that he could make decisions essential to his kingdom. Whether or not his subjects could see his outfits was important, as it allowed him to separate the smart from the stupid and to see who had been placed in positions that they did not deserve. The emperor, "dressed" in imaginary cloth, walked naked through the streets of the town, exposing much more about himself than about his townspeople.

It is my fervent hope that no preachers are crawling with spiritual lice or wearing any version of the emperor's suit. This poem and this story are, however, important cautionary tales. They teach the importance of knowing ourselves well and of assessing ourselves through the eyes of those who surround us. What is our view of ourselves? Does it match the opinions that others have of us? Do we see ourselves as others do? And, if not, what might we learn from their perceptions?

In other words, do preachers see themselves as we see them?

learn from your reflection

Oh, that God would give us the very smallest of gifts
To see ourselves as others see us.[2]

A brief study of the science of reflection provides assistance in understanding how we see ourselves (and gives us a way to consider how we might be seen by others). When rays of light, thrown from a set of focal points, converge on mirrored glass, we are able to see our reflections. That is the job of mirrors, those polished surfaces that divert light based on the laws of reflection. Dating back to the sixteenth century, the earliest mirrors were stationary household objects in which wealthy persons could view themselves. When seventeenth-century mercury processes facilitated the development of handheld mirrors, the appeal of the visible self-image reached the masses.

In this culture, people clearly tend to revel in their self-images. We check ourselves to see if, on a daily basis, our reflections match our perception of ourselves. We assess whether we're having a good or a bad "hair day" and whether our clothes hide our physical flaws. We rate ourselves against our standards for ourselves. "My, my, my," we say, "you sure look good today!" And our mirrors tell the truth, even when the truth is ugly.

We all know people whose self-perception differs greatly from how they are viewed by others. We know those who, like the hat-wearing, louse-ridden churchgoer or the naked emperor, have no idea how they appear to others. "Mirror, mirror, on the wall, who's the fairest of them all?" asks the vain queen in a well-known fairy tale. But unlike the mirrors in fairy tales, our mirrors don't talk to us; they cannot make us what we are not or tell us only what we want to hear.

It is important that we recognize ourselves, both the good and the bad, when we see our reflections in the mirror. I sometimes worry that some preachers are unable to see themselves realistically. Some preachers appear to have elevated themselves to emperor status. Some forget that their roles are less important than their responsibility to preach God's Word, pastor God's people, serve community needs, and manage the business of the church so that it is well equipped for kingdom building. No matter how preachers view themselves, no matter how grand their "bonnets," if their souls are not in order, their "lice" are bound to show. If they do, those of us in the pews will see them and become concerned about the capacity of the preacher to lead us to the gate of God's kingdom. The mirror image reflects the truth; it shows preachers the reflection of a child of God, not of one who is a god.

through a glass, darkly

For now we see through a glass, darkly; but then face to face: now I know in part; but then shall I know even as also I am known. (1 Corinthians 13:12)

Our reflections necessarily differ somewhat from who we actually are; they are, in fact, the optical reverse of our exact image. Left is right and right is left, always. Life shows us reflections as well. In addition to the self-assessment provided for our eyes when we look in the mirror, we look for our reflections in the faces and responses of others. They, too, are somewhat filtered.

Human reflections are seen through experience and emotion, through memory and the meaning that we attach to certain people at certain points in time. Parishioners serve (or should serve) as mirrors for preachers, as emotive reflections

95

of how they sense God moving through the preacher into realms of spiritual meaning in their own lives. In their eyes, as in the mirror on the wall, it may be a good day or a bad day for the preacher. Preachers, like everyone else, must learn to live with disappointment, with a less than stellar preaching moment, and they can take encouragement from the certain knowledge that God speaks eloquently even when they don't.

Of course, as I've repeated in various ways in this book, it's not just about how the preacher preaches; it's also about the preacher's demeanor in the pulpit and the way the preacher pastors. As we have noted, a preacher who is pastor does a great service to parishioners. It brings us face to face with you in a relationship that builds up the kingdom of God.

remember our humanity
Love is, above all, the gift of oneself.[3]

Though we ask that you see yourself as we see you, preacher, we in the pew must admit that parishioners sometimes are difficult. Tending to ignore the planks in our own eyes, we often are unforgiving of the specks in your eyes that we view as pastoral shortcomings. Iyanla Vanzant discussed this phenomenon:

> When we become angry, upset or disappointed with someone, we forget the good they have done. We seem to think people must prove themselves to us again and again. If ever they fail to live up to our expectations, we are quick to voice our dismay. The ancient Africans taught that if a person is good to you, you must forever speak good of them. They believed the good always outlives the not so good. In order to keep the good flowing, you must speak

of it. The ancestors taught that we must honor those who helped us when we were in need, regardless of what they do now. We must honor those who taught us, even if we no longer use the lessons. We must remember with a kind word the road someone else has paved for us, no matter where or how they travel now. Everything we receive in life is food for our growth. If we eat from the plate, we must give thanks. Remembering without that food, at that time, we may have starved.[4]

We give thanks for you, preacher, and for the growth you have encouraged in us, using the gift of God's Word, without which we may have starved.

learn from us
Get real![5]

Dr. Phil McGraw, whose motto is "Get real!," has gained enormous popularity because he gives commonsense responses, backed by psychological theory, to our problems. One of his important "life lessons" is that we teach others how to treat us. If we are in challenging relationships, we must assess what permission we have given others to treat us that way. This entire book is an attempt to say, "These are the problems that parishioners see occurring in the pulpit. Listen to what we have to say. Learn from us. Work with us to make our churches all that they can and should be."

lead us, guide us
I am weak and I need Thy strength and power
To help me o'er my weakest hour.
Help me through the darkness, Thy face to see,
Lead me, O Lord, lead me.[6]

We in the pew expect that preachers, as part of their calling, have been granted the gift of discernment, the grace-filled vision to see the unseen and to perceive what is in the human heart. The purpose of salvation is deliverance. Although our personal salvation as parishioners ultimately is based upon our own spiritual work, we tend to believe that it's the preachers' job to open doors that facilitate our salvation. With so many wounded hearts coming to Christ, the need for salvation and deliverance is evident in our churches. If, as so many of us have been taught, God grants discernment so that we can use what we have seen to bring him glory, then preachers must use this gift well. If the work of the pulpit somehow becomes something other than glorifying Christ for the purpose of saving our souls, then we must all fall to our knees and pray.

look to the pew for confirmation
Well I said I wouldn't tell it to a livin' soul,
How He brought salvation and He made me whole,
But I found I couldn't hide such a love as Jesus did impart.
Oh, He made me laugh and He made me cry,
Set my sinful soul on fire, Hallelujah!
When God dips His love in my heart.[7]

We want to love you, pastor. Make it easy for us.

see what we see
I stepped on the rock, the rock was sound.
The love of God came streaming down.
The reason I know He saved my soul,
I dug down deep and found pure gold.[8]

What do we in the pew see when we look at you in the pulpit?

- We see persons called of God.
- We see men and women of God, who have responsibility for the management of church programs and ministry to the lives of a congregation of believers.
- We see preachers who must weekly prepare to bring God's Word.
- We see ministers who must model Christian lives for us.
- We see preachers, inspired by God's Word, aided by the Holy Spirit, and encouraged by the love of Christ as it is made evident in their own lives.
- We see pastors, sensitive to our needs, who can assist us with our spiritual challenges and pray with us concerning Christian approaches to daily decisions.
- We see human beings with feelings and failings.

And with you, seeing you as we hope you see yourselves, we seek to become pure gold.

thoughts from the pulpit

Preacher's Prayer: Holy God, I seek your face. Lead me from my paths of personal darkness into the light of your love, into the place where I can do your work, for your purpose, among your people. I praise your name. Amen.

Pastor's Promise: I promise to be available to you, my parishioners, so that we may learn and grow together as one body in Christ. I promise to see you as people who, like me, always strive to do God's will but sometimes fail. I promise to use my knowledge of God to help you, not to alienate you through use of fear tactics. I promise to model Christian behavior in my life, so that you can see in me someone who strives for good.

Because I am flawed and sometimes fail, I ask your promise of patience for my humanity and forgiveness for my faults. As we walk this path together, let us ask God's assistance in keeping our promises to ourselves and to each other.

Minister's Message: We must work together in a process of continuous assessment that teaches us what is required for our growth and development as preacher and people—all of us, God's children.

thoughts from the pew

Parishioners' Prayer: Dear Lord, let us, as pastor and people, be sensitive to each other's needs. May we, as parishioners, provide support for our pastor, understanding the challenges and blessings of this vital role. Help our pastor minister to our needs as well, seeing in us partners in this essential work, the building your kingdom. You need all hands, Lord, and we are here. Amen.

Parishioners' Plea: Pastor, honor us with your preparation, preaching, and presentation. As you see and respond to our needs, we will see and respond to yours. We view the relationship of pastor and people as a blessed one, and we look forward to our journey together.

NOTES

1. Robert Burns, "To a Louse: On Seeing One on a Lady's Bonnet in Church." The verse translates into modern English as, "Oh, that God would give us the very smallest of gifts / To see ourselves as others see us" (http://www.robertburns.plus.com [accessed September 14, 2002]).

2. Ibid.

3. Jean Anouilh, http://www.quotationspage.com (accessed September 14, 2002).

4. Iyanla Vanzant, *Acts of Faith: Daily Meditations for People of Color* (New York: Fireside Books, 1993), August 1.

5. Motto of psychologist and television personality Dr. Phil McGraw.

6. Doris M. Akers, "Lead Me, Guide Me," in *African American Heritage Hymnal,* ed. Delores Carpenter and Nolan E. Williams Jr. (Chicago: GIA Publications, 2001), 474. Copyright © by GIA Publications, Inc., Chicago, Illinois. All rights reserved. Used with permission.

7. Ralph Hill and Bobby Atkins, "When God Dips His Pen of Love in My Heart" (Tompaul Music, BMI).

8. William Herbert Brewster, "Jesus Is All," (Chappell & Company, 1949).

CHAPTER 10

be satisfied

Take a stand, take a stand, take a stand,
If I never ever see you any more.
Take a stand, take a stand, take a stand,
Till I meet you on the other shore.[1]

AFTER ALL IS SAID AND DONE, THE JUDGE OF PREACHERLY PASSION and vision, pastoral care and concern, and ministerial skill is God alone. But as God's earthly servant, you the preacher, if you are confident that you have given your best to God and his people, must be satisfied with your efforts.

model self-esteem and self-satisfaction

O satisfy us early with thy mercy; that we may rejoice and be glad all our days. (Psalm 90:14)

Too many preachers suffer from a fear that by bringing excellence through other preachers into their pulpits they will show the pew their own shortcomings. On the contrary, we in the pew will be excited to learn from preachers with different perspectives, saints who speak with different voices, and persons whose life experiences vary significantly from yours. If you bring to us a variety of voices, we will learn that you are comfortable in *yourself*, and that will be an important lesson for us to be satisfied with *ourselves*. In an age when poor self-esteem runs rampant, this is an essential lesson to learn from the pulpit.

satisfaction shows
"There is no greater joy than knowing that I have not lived in vain. I have not preached in vain. I have not moved from town to town and job to job in vain.... I have not labored in vain, sweated in vain, prayed in vain, suffered in vain. Now I know how the old people felt when they sang, ... 'I wouldn't take nothing for my journey now.'"[2]

One preacher I heard give a sermon for a position as pastor referred to himself nearly thirty times as bishop from the pulpit. He then made the point in his sermon that when Jesus was called king by his followers, he refused the appellation. This young preacher told the congregation that the reason that Christ was able to ignore the title of king was that he, Christ, was comfortable with who he was. Those comfortable with who they are, the preacher said, did not need titles. He immediately followed this point with, "Can the bishop get an Amen?"—not recognizing that, in so doing, he was labeling himself as someone insecure with who *he* was. This "bishop"[3] signalled loudly from the pulpit that he was not satisfied with himself, and in this, and through the number of times that he trumpeted his own title from the pulpit, invalidated the message of self-esteem that he thought he was illustrating in his sermon.

In an era when there is so much much to challenge the self-esteem of parishioners, it is important that preachers demonstrate strength of character from the pulpit. This does not mean that we want to see false shows of bravado, because we value the knowledge that you are human and struggle too. Evidence of who you are and how God works in and through you is something that we value learning through your sermons. Honesty wins our hearts. Satisfaction shows.

build god's army

We are soldiers in the army,
We have to fight although we have to cry.
We've got to hold up the blood-stained banner,
We have to hold it up until we die.[4]

Self-satisfaction is, to some degree, related to the choices that we make about how to live our lives. At the Christian discipleship institute in July 2002 at the Metropolitan Baptist Church in Washington, D.C., Rev. Romal Tune[5] taught "Crossroads: The Choices We Make," a class on strategies for keeping God first in our decision making. A military veteran of the Gulf War, he described for the class the training of Special Forces teams. To make sure that they are highly prepared to fight in the most torturous conditions, these elite soldiers train their bodies to withstand extremes. However, their most important training is psychological: they have power over the enemy if they steel their minds to the task of protecting their country at all costs. The culmination of their training blends their physical prowess and their mental toughness. At night, wearing forty-pound backpacks, they are flown to a great height and dropped into the ocean. They must swim to shore and run across the finish line. They are consummate soldiers under extreme stress.

Preaching should do the same for those in the pew; it should serve as Special Forces training for spiritual warriors in the army of God. Preaching should so prepare us for spiritual battle that when we are dropped, heavily weighted, into our seas of difficulty, we have the strength to swim to shore and the faith to run toward the finish line, not knowing when we'll cross it, but assured that Jesus is with us every step and that our pastor is praying us through.

wait on the word

But they that wait upon the LORD *shall renew their strength;*
they shall mount up with wings as eagles; they shall run,
and not be weary; and they shall walk, and not faint.
(Isaiah 40:31)

Those who wait on the Lord will renew their strength, and preachers must, through their behavior and preaching, help parishioners learn as much as possible from this personal obligation to Christ. We need our preachers to be dedicated to the creation of meaningful worship experiences that elevate the role of preaching to high art and, as a result, provide intelligent and meaningful inspiration to all who hear them. We need preachers who will prepare us for spiritual warfare and assist our development into a powerful army for the Lord. Preachers who accomplish these goals certainly can feel satisfied that they have engaged in efforts worthy of their station, meaningful to God's people, and pleasing to Christ.

sit down sometimes

I have fought a good fight, I have finished my course,
I have kept the faith. (2 Timothy 4:7)

This recommendation regarding finding satisfaction in your work as a preacher is simply this: sit down from time to time.

Sometimes the preacher needs to be preached *to* rather than being the one who preaches. Every once in a while the preacher should hear for himself or herself the immutable, unassailable Word of God. The preacher should occasionally sit in the pew as part of the congregation of Christian believers (with persons from their own coasts), a seat that acknowledges that the preacher, too, is a sinner saved by grace and has need of some silent moments to just *be* in the context of worship, in the presence of the Lord. Sometimes the preacher must simply sit down.[6]

preach as if you have only one sermon to preach

With my whole heart, Lord I will sing to Thee
With my whole heart, I'll make melody.
I'll focus on Thy glory
So I can come before Thee
With my whole heart.[7]

Rev. Dr. H. Beecher Hicks Jr. urges preachers to preach the authentic gospel:

> I want to talk today on one sermon to preach. Nearly a quarter of a century ago, a Scottish-born preacher, pastor of the Madison Avenue Presbyterian Church in New York City, wrote a book entitled, *The Sons of Anak,* a book which I dare say most of you have not had a chance yet to read. In the main, David H. C. Reed's book is a work of numerous sermons, which did not make the best seller list then and would not make the best seller list now. I bring this work to your attention, however, because of a challenge which captivated my spirit in the closing lines of the concluding paragraphs of his writing. One preacher spoke to another and simply suggested that it is possible for a preacher to spend the

whole of his ministry and never preach a word of the authentic gospel.[8]

Hicks goes on to exhort preachers that it is vital that they must, in every sermon on every Sunday, preach as if they have only one sermon to preach, pray as if they have in them only one final prayer, interact with their parishioners as if they might never again see them, understanding that in each moment, God is expecting of them their best efforts, and they dare not waste one precious moment. "One ought be careful, I tell you," Hicks says, "what one does in the name of preaching."

be satisfied

Satisfied, satisfied, satisfied,
If I never ever see you any more.
Satisfied, satisfied, satisfied,
Till I meet you on the other shore.[9]

Finally, dear preachers, it is important to remember that you in the pulpit and we in the pew are partners in the preaching venture. God's grace and mercy guides us through it, his love sustains us in it, and his blessings follow us after it. If we give praise to God, he will be pleased, and together we, his children, can turn our eyes toward heaven and raise our voices in adoration and our hands in praise. Together, we can be satisfied.

thoughts from the pulpit

Preacher's Prayer: Dear God, when I was hungry, you fed me. When I was without hope, you propped me up. What I have needed, you have provided. For these things, I give you thanks. Help me, in the failings of my flesh and my faith, to be satisfied with who I am, with what I have done, with how I have tended the sheep whose care you have commended to me, and for what you have done for me, in me, with me, and through me. Grant me strength, I pray, for the living of these days, for the tending of your vineyard, and for the ability to do your will. From everlasting to everlasting, you are Christ our Lord; world without end. Amen.

Pastor's Promise: As God has taught me, so I will teach you. As God has answered my prayers, so I will pray for you. As God has lifted me up, so I will seek to support you. I will seek to preach every sermon as if I have only one sermon to preach, as if it is my very last. I will strive to do my best in presenting to you the undiluted gospel and the Word of God. As I tend to you as your pastor, I will strive to understand the components of your needs and help you to be satisfied with what God has given you.

Minister's Message: In my ministry I will strive to do my best, ever prayerful that my efforts will meet the goals that God has set for me and fulfill the promises that I have made to him. I will fight the good fight and keep the faith, praying that there will be reserved for me the crown of righteousness, life, and glory.

thoughts from the pew

Parishioners' Prayer: Gracious God, we learn from the hymnist, *"If when you give the best of your service; Telling the world that the Savior is come; Be not dismayed when men don't believe you; He'll understand; And say, 'Well done.'"*[10] We pray that you will be praised through our preacher's ministry, so that you will be pleased to say to (him or her), "Well done, good and faithful servant! You have been faithful with a few things; I will put you in charge of many things. Come and share your master's happiness!" We thank you for our preacher and give praise to you. Amen.

Parishioners' Plea: Pastor, preach well, behave sincerely and lovingly, and administer well the field that the Lord has given you to tend. We understand that in each sermon you are trying to preach as if it were your only opportunity to teach, to pray, to praise and glorify God. We understand that you are working hard to create a church that functions as a corporate body capable of building God's kingdom on earth. We understand that you sometimes may struggle with the partner in you. But we are with you, and we love you. We are partners with you in this Jesus venture; we are the Special Forces in the Lord's army. Well done, God's preacher, well done. We, also God's servants, are here to do our part. We love you, as God loves us. And we will thrive because God's kingdom on earth will be built with our hands. It is our task. Let us begin.

NOTES

1. African American spiritual, "Meet You on the Other Shore."

2. Ella Mitchell, "Therefore" in *Fire in the Well: Sermons by Ella and Henry Mitchell*, Edited by Jacqueline B. Glass (Valley Forge, Pa.: Judson Press, 2003), 52.

3. Further complicating this sermon was the fact that this preacher was Baptist and that the Baptist faith does not have an official role for bishops. An important and essential tenet of the Baptist faith is that each Baptist church is an independent, autonomous entity. A consequence of this independence is that there is no oversight body

that organizes the autonomous churches and assigns bishops to them. It is thought instead, since one translation of the word "bishop" is "teacher," that each Baptist pastor is, in effect, a bishop. However, some persons have broken away to form a component of bishops within a Baptist group known as the Full Gospel, a group that is controversial within the Baptist faith.

4. Gospel Hymn, "We Are Soldiers in the Army," in *African American Heritage Hymnal,* ed. Delores Carpenter and Nolan E. Williams Jr. (Chicago: GIA Publications, 2001), 488. Copyright © by GIA Publications, Inc., Chicago, Illinois. All rights reserved. Used with permission.

5. Rev Romal Tune is Minister of Congregational Growth and Development at Nineteenth Street Baptist Church, Washington, D.C., and National Senior Organizer for African American Church Programs, People for the American Way.

6. For preachers to feel comfortable acting on this recommendation, they must be very comfortable with themselves. That comfort allows them to invite other preachers into their pulpits and to place themselves in the pews for a moment, joining with their parishioners for a different perspective of worship in which they listen rather than speak.

7. Nolan Williams Jr. (author and composer), "With My Whole Heart," New-J Publishing, a division of NEWorks Publications, 1995.

8. Rev. Dr. H. Beecher Hicks Jr., Metropolitan Baptist Church, Washington, D.C., March 23, 2003, 11:00 a.m. service.

9. African American spiritual, "Meet You on the Other Shore."

10. Lucie E. Campbell, "He'll Understand and Say, 'Well Done,'" in *African American Heritage Hymnal,* ed. Delores Carpenter and Nolan E. Williams Jr. (Chicago: GIA Publications, 2001), 413. Copyright © by GIA Publications, Inc., Chicago, Illinois. All rights reserved. Used with permission.